Praise for

At the heart of every successful ᴄ..ᴛ ᴄᴦ prise are people who build trust—with their staff, customers and partners. Trust, as Lyn and Donna suggest, is 'a feeling, not a behaviour... helping us to form bonds at an emotional level'. The best way to build trust is to be authentic in all the ways we interact with each other, and this book is full of helpful tips, thoughtful suggestions and compelling success stories. This succinct but detailed review of what works in building and sustaining trust, which in turn creates and sustains successful companies, will be helpful for sole traders, small businesses and giant concerns.

Kate Davies
Chief Executive
Notting Hill Housing Trust

A totally different approach to all other management publications, this book helps the reader appreciate the huge value of his or her leadership potential.

Andrew Haworth
Managing Director
Bartle Hall Lancashire

Trusted is a wonderful mix of corporate best practice, pulling together some amazing knowledge and delivered in an easy-going, well-structured manner, by two fantastic business consultants. A great read and tool to keep and refer back to!

Mark Moseley
Managing Director
Band Hatton Button Solicitors

Huge congratulations on writing a fabulous book! I learnt so much from reading it that will help me both personally and professionally. I love the credibility sleuth and credibility thief. This is a very practical and applicable resource and I like the use of diagrams and case studies throughout the book.

Lucy Barton
Senior Membership Value Propositions Manager
Nationwide Building Society

It was so refreshing to read *Trusted* as a development book that addresses the physical, mental, and emotional sides of my sense of self. *Trusted* has a business head and is full of heart. I recommend it to anyone looking to strengthen commercially while remaining at peace with your inner self.

Sarah Windrum, CEO, Emerald Group

Trusted

The human approach to building outstanding client relationships in a digitised world

by
Lyn Bromley &
Donna Whitbrook

First published in Great Britain by

Practical Inspiration Publishing, 2017

© Lyn Bromley & Donna Whitbrook, 2017

The moral rights of the authors have been asserted

ISBN (print): 978-1-910056-55-4
ISBN (ebook): 978-1-910056-54-7 (Kindle)
ISBN (ebook): 978-1-910056-74-5 (ePub)

Practical Inspiration
PUBLISHING

With love to our families for their endless support xx

Contents

Welcome

Welcome to **Trusted**.

On a rather beautiful summer's day, while developing bespoke programmes for our clients, we were enthusing about the experiences we've had throughout our working lives, and about our desire to inspire others to achieve excellence. We made the decision there and then to write Trusted.

We distilled our combined 60 years of professional experience and our passion for developing people in order to create, research and bring together the information in this book. We also interviewed 22 hand-picked experts, and look forward to sharing their stories with you.

Leaders, individuals, and managers can all use the concepts and advice in this book. If you are a senior leader, fantastic—you have the power to transform your organisation by implementing the strategies outlined.

If you are an individual or a manager, great—you can use our advice for personal or team development. We have seen the benefits of these concepts in both large corporations and SMEs.

The book is divided into five key sections, and we invite you to read them sequentially as the content will make more sense that way.

We hope you enjoy reading Trusted and use it as an ongoing reference tool!

Lyn Bromley and Donna Whitbrook, October 2017.

'Face-to-face over coffee is worth over a thousand tweets.'

– Mark Weinberger, global CEO, EY

Introduction

In a world of digitised interactions, connecting on a human level is more valuable than ever. It's time to step back and realise how important it is to build outstanding business relationships. By focusing on the skills that affect the client's experience and the company's ability to deliver excellent service, your organisation can gain a competitive advantage. Organisations will benefit from improved profits, higher employee retention, a better reputation and sustained growth.

Several forces are making connecting on a personal level more relevant in today's world.

- Millennials continue to receive bad press regarding their inability to converse and are being cited as unable to communicate effectively, build relationships and have meaningful face-to-face interactions. But these issues are not as age specific as the media leads us to believe. They are equally as relevant to older individuals, as well as leaders and organisations. Do we really want to move forward with faceless interactions?

- Our 'one-click' world has changed buyers' expectations. We all expect interactions with organisations to be quick and easy. We are becoming 'Uber's children', getting whatever we want almost instantly. This increases our expectations of all interactions.

- We have less tolerance for things going wrong, and are much more likely to complain. And complaints, of course, can be shared at the push of a button.

- New competitors are flooding almost every market. This is driven by certain lower barriers of entry due to both globalisation and the technological revolution. It is therefore an opportunity to differentiate through service offerings and stand out in this crowded market.

Against this changing landscape, our clients often ask us to help them deliver 'world-class service' or 'service excellence'. As part of this work, we ask for feedback on what these terms mean to them. Each client has a slightly different definition based on his or her own experiences, standards and values. Albeit, common themes come out.

The theme that clients regularly discuss is a focus on PEOPLE. People within organisations are either great ambassadors or brand saboteurs. We will be exploring what it means to be a great ambsssador or a brand saboteur in more detail throughout the book.

Some of you may not want to reach the dizzy heights of being a world-class organisation, but you can certainly learn from them to help you to achieve your growth objectives.

Focusing on behavioural and service-aptitude skills allows you to differentiate yourself from your competition.

We have all heard the phrase 'people buy from people', but so many companies fail to develop their people to be the best advocates for their brand and to build a strong people-based culture.

Sir Richard Branson, founder of Virgin Group, has an approach we admire:

'Train people well enough so they can leave, treat them well enough so they don't want to. If you look after your staff, they'll look after your customers. It's that simple.'

What factors prevent an organisation from developing outstanding business relationships?

- Declining customer or client service
- Inappropriate tone of voice across all channels of communication
- Lack of awareness of the importance of non-verbal communication
- Inconsistent behaviour
- The absence of non-negotiable standards
- Toxic cultures
- The paying of lip service to values
- Declining face-to-face communication skills
- Lack of understanding of professional image
- Inability to interact (which prevents relationship-building skills)
- Closed mindsets (not open to new ideas or ways of doing things)
- Lack of respect for colleagues and clients
- Inability to adapt to the changing business environment

Many organisations exhibit some or all of the above behaviours and issues.

Through our experience in helping our clients solve these problems, we have developed a model that addresses each of these issues in turn and delivers a measurable increase of trust in both internal and external professional relationships.

The T-Spot Model

The model consists of five core areas that must align with the organisation's culture and values.

When all of the model's elements have been embedded, your people will be great advocates for the business, they will deliver excellent service and they will be trusted by each other, your prospects and your clients.

We've seen how organisations' cultures are strengthened and how their values become more meaningful after the model has been implemented.

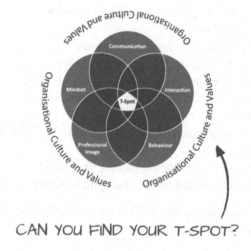

CAN YOU FIND YOUR T-SPOT?

T-Spot Model, © First Impressions

Mastering our mindsets, becoming great communicators, developing excellent interaction skills, being consistent in our behaviour and having an awareness of the impact of our professional image will lead us to the T-Spot in the centre of the model. The T-Spot represents our ability to build outstanding client relationships. It's where trusted relationships reside.

Of course, this won't happen overnight. Creating cultural change takes time.

In their book *Corporate Culture and Performance*, John Kotter and James Heskett show that 'corporate culture can have a significant impact on a firm's long-term economic performance'. They found that organisations with cultures that emphasised customers, stockholders and employees and had leadership at all levels outperformed companies that did not by a huge margin. Over an 11-year period, these organisations showed increases in the following areas: revenue by 682%, workforce by 166%, stock prices by 901% and net income by 756%.

Identify the small improvements that can be implemented and embedded. We advocate using the aggregation of marginal gains concept as a systematic and continuous approach.

Marginal gains

When looking at what makes organisations world class, we use Sir David Brailsford's analogy. Brailsford is a British cycling coach and general manager of Team Sky. In 2010, when he was appointed performance director for Team Sky, Brailsford was asked to find a winner for the Tour de France. He believes in the concept of aggregation of marginal gains. As he explains, 'If you improve every area by just 1%, and there is 1% margin for improvement in everything you do, those small gains would add up to remarkable improvement'.

Team Sky started looking for improvements. Initially focusing on nutrition, training, and the ergonomics of the bike seat and tyres, they identified some results. Then Team Sky looked for 1% improvements in areas that others had overlooked, and identified a type of pillow that ensured the best sleep. Riders began taking this pillow everywhere. They were also educated on the best way to wash their hands to avoid infection and illness.

Brailsford was confident that the marginal gains strategy would increase Team Sky's potential to win the Tour de France in five years. And in fact, they won in two years rather than five. Bradley Wiggins won in 2012, and Chris Froome won the following year. Under Brailsford's leadership, the Great Britain Cycling Team also led the cycling medal tables at the 2008 and 2012 Olympic Games. The cycling team continued to improve, winning multiple world championships in road, track, BMX and mountain bike racing.

We should never assume that small changes are insignificant. Consider interest. You start with a small amount, but when left to grow and multiply, it soon adds up. Albert Einstein reportedly said that 'the most powerful force in the universe is compound interest'.

How do we use the aggregation of marginal gains concept to help us to find the T-Spot?

The key is to make small changes every day. Get in the habit of focusing on improvement, even by very small margins.

'Almost every habit that you have, good or bad, is the result of many small decisions over time.' – *Sir Dave Brailsford*

AGGREGATION OF MARGINAL GAINS
☐ 1% Improvement
☐ 1% Decline

Time ⟶

Adapted from *The Slight Edge*, by Jeff Olson

At the far left of the graph, there is little difference between a 1% improvement and a 1% decline, but compounded over time these small changes lead to a much larger and more significant gap.

Brailsford explains the power of the culture that marginal gains create. 'Everyone is looking for ways to improve, whether individually or as a group. If an entire organisation is constantly striving to improve, it's going to create a positive and dynamic culture.'

And according to Brailsford, the approach is just as applicable in the business world. 'I think there are ample opportunities in the corporate realm to apply the marginal gains approach.'

Things to look out for

We have developed some simple icons to make it easier for you to navigate the book, and to highlight significant points.

When you see this icon, head to our website for additional downloadable material, including a workbook. **www.firstimpressions.uk.com/trusted**

We'll be posing questions to pause and reflect upon. We have also included all of the 'Pause' questions in a downloadable workbook with space for you to write your thoughts: **www.firstimpressions.uk.com/trusted**

Meet our credibility sleuth. At the end of each chapter we will summarise the key learning points for you. This icon highlights the 1% marginal gains.

Finally, meet our credibility thief. We need to keep him out of your business! This icon will show you the things that could be damaging your credibility and reducing your organisation's profits.

Starting the journey

Some elements of the model will resonate with you more than the others. We recommend that you start by making your 1% marginal gains in these areas first.

Enjoy the journey, and please share your success stories with us. Use the hashtag #findyourtspot on social media.

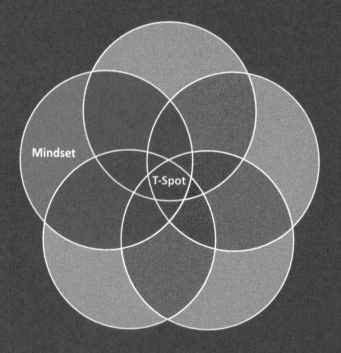

Mindset

T-Spot

'Know yourself and you will win all battles.'

—Sun Tzu, philosopher

Seizing control of your mindset is one
of the most powerful and fundamental
actions you can take to achieve personal
and professional success.

Mindset

Our own experience and research has shown us that in order to build outstanding relationships and deliver outstanding client service, we must first manage our mindset.

Most people do not manage their mindset—they are not aware that it can even be managed. But the most successful leaders, sportspeople and clinicians know that managing their mindset sets them up for success.

'Whether you think you can or you think you can't, you're right.' – *Henry Ford, founder of the Ford Motor Company*

The culture of the organisation we're working within can also influence our mindset. Processes that do not allow employees to feel trusted and valued can have a significant impact on mindset. Whether people are trusted or treated with suspicion, they will live up to the expectation.

'Beliefs drive attitudes which affect behaviours.' - *Unknown*

Growth mindset

Dr Carol S. Dweck, professor of psychology at Stanford University and leading researcher in the field of motivation, has spent decades researching achievement and success, and has determined that there are two types of mindset: fixed and growth. She also determined the power of mindset and the profound affect it can have on our lives.

Prior to her research, she held the belief that we couldn't get smarter; whatever we were born with was what we had. Through her research, she has discredited her original belief and proven that we can become smarter.

Do you have a fixed or growth mindset?

People with a fixed mindset:

- believe that intelligence is fixed and their qualities are carved in stone
- avoid challenges
- give up easily
- don't see the value of effort
- avoid negative feedback
- are threatened by others' success, and
- shy away from challenges for fear of being exposed.

People with a growth mindset:

- believe that intelligence can be developed and their qualities can be cultivated through effort
- embrace challenges—in fact, they relish challenge
- see effort as a path to mastering a skill
- learn from criticism
- incorporate learning and get inspiration from others' success, and
- believe that we don't all have the same talents and abilities but that we can all grow through hard work, mentorship and perseverance.

Depending on which mindset we operate in, we either narrow our world or widen it. Those with fixed mindsets narrow their world to appear as though they are achieving, whereas those with growth mindsets open up their world so they can look for opportunities and challenges, allowing them to grow.

Many people have elements of both mindsets, and different mindsets for different areas. For example, a person could have great social skills but think she is incapable of standing up and delivering a presentation for a group. Someone could have a great business mind but think he is unable to master new gadgets.

Beliefs are powerful. We do have a choice; we can change our mindsets if we want to.

What you can do to move to a growth mindset

- Raise your awareness—simply understanding that you have two mindsets enables you to challenge your thinking and can produce incredible results.

- Acknowledge that we all have elements of fixed and growth mindsets—don't beat yourself up; it's what makes us human. By embracing this, you can start to notice how often your fixed mindset creeps in. I (Lyn) think I can't sing, and I (Donna) think I can't draw. In reality, we know that if we were motivated to overcome these limiting beliefs, we could enrol in singing and art classes, and we know we could improve. Our motivation to do so is clearly low; otherwise, we would already have taken steps to rectify these perceived shortcomings.

- Become aware of triggers—know when your fixed-mindset persona shows up.
  ◊ Perhaps at a networking event you meet someone in your industry who appears more confident and polished. How do you feel? Do you shrink in comparison, and is your mind telling you that you can never be as good?
  ◊ How about when you lose a prospect during a pitch—do you blame yourself? And does this knock your confidence and ability to win future pitches?

◊ How do you handle it when you receive a complaint? Do you become defensive?

◊ Maybe you've received negative feedback during a personal development review. Do you feel uncomfortable and maybe choose to ignore the feedback? Do you dislike your manager a little for giving the feedback?

◊ Or perhaps a colleague has been praised for doing something well. Are you looking for ways to discredit what he or she has done to make yourself feel better?

• Name your fixed-mindset persona—this might seem a little odd, but bear with us. It works well in practice.

◊ We were talking about pricing with one of our clients (a high-end business, so not the cheapest in their sector). A senior employee argued that they would not attract new business as their price point was too high. Her fixed-mindset persona, whom she had named Margaret, had taken over. Her tone changed and so did her style of communication, which became very direct. When challenged, she became even more direct and defensive. Another senior colleague in the room responded, saying, 'When Margaret comes out in this way, it impacts the group's ability to move forward with the discussion because she is so closed off'. Another colleague bravely spoke up at this point: 'When Margaret comes out, I feel that I can't get my point out and I just fall silent. This is Violet, my fixed-mindset persona. She shrinks and feels intimidated and tongue-tied'. These revelations allowed the group to continue the discussion. Once they understood each other's triggers and personas, they were able to move past them and identify the real barriers to winning new business.

- Educate your mindset—once you have identified your triggers and have named your fixed-mindset persona, take your persona on the journey to grow your mindset. Later in this section, we will explore a number of ways you could do this. For example, you could find a mentor to support you, work with a coach to help you develop, ask for constructive feedback (perhaps 360-degree feedback if you're a manager), listen to what your clients say about you, or work on positive affirmations and visualisations and on removing limiting beliefs.

Managing your mindset is not a one-off event. It takes time and continual effort to flip the switch from fixed mindset to growth mindset. But once you've done so, seemingly insurmountable challenges will be easier to navigate.

How you can inspire your team to have a growth mindset

- Promote problem-solving when failure occurs.
- Praise teamwork and effort, not just outcomes.
- Lead by example: walk the talk.
- Encourage the team to share and talk about how they have overcome challenges.
- Show vulnerability as a leader and allow team members to show vulnerability too.
- Celebrate team wins—again, not just the outcome but also the process.
- Encourage and empower the team to ask better questions.
- Place a high value on learning (for everyone, including leaders).
- Encourage the team to obtain feedback from clients and promote peer-to-peer feedback.
- Coach employees on how to benefit from feedback.
- Encourage staff to embrace new challenges and to step outside their comfort zones.

- Encourage healthy and open debate and conflict. This avoids groupthink, where everyone agrees with an egotistical leader and nobody is able to challenge his or her viewpoints.

 Can you identify whether your mindset is fixed or growth in different circumstances?

Emotional intelligence

Emotional intelligence is the capacity to be aware of, control and express your emotions, and to handle interpersonal relationships judiciously and empathetically.

Emotional intelligence, also referred to as emotional quotient (EI or EQ), is broken down into four categories:

- self-awareness—your ability to perceive your emotions and understand your tendency to act in certain ways in given situations
- social awareness—your ability to understand others' emotions (what others are thinking and feeling)
- self-management—your ability to use awareness of your emotions to stay flexible and direct your behaviour positively and constructively, and
- relationship management—your ability to use your awareness of your emotions and those of others to manage interactions successfully.

It's our behaviour that puts people at ease (or produces the opposite effect). Good behavioural skills enable us to build and maintain personal and professional relationships founded on confidence and trust. The following are a few self-development strategies to increase your EI:

- make self-reflection a daily habit to raise your awareness of your current mindset
- pay attention to your behaviour
- practise greeting people by name

- listen appreciatively in conversations
- aim to respond rather than react
- go for a ten-minute tour of your work environment each day with the sole aim of connecting with people, and
- observe social interactions between other people.

Decades of research show that 70% of the time, emotional intelligence is the critical factor when people with average IQs outperform those with high IQs. And 90% of top performers have high emotional intelligence scores. The research also states that emotional intelligence is responsible for 58% of your job performance. People with higher emotional intelligence earn higher salaries than those with lower emotional intelligence.

But high emotional intelligence won't do a thing for you unless you are genuine with it. People don't accept signs of emotional intelligence at face value; they want to see congruence with gestures, body language and actions, too.

As research scientist Christina Fong says, co-workers 'are not just mindless automatons—they think about the emotions they see and care whether they are sincere or manipulative'.

Her research reports that leaders are more effective at motivating people when they inspire trust and admiration through their actions and not just their words.

According to Dr Travis Bradberry, author of *Emotional Intelligence 2.0*, 'Genuine people don't try to make people like them. It's not that they don't care whether or not other people will like them, but simply they are not going to let that get in the way of doing the right thing. They are willing to make unpopular decisions and to take unpopular positions if that's what needs to be done. People catch on to your attitude quickly and are more attracted to the right attitude than what or how many people you know.'

How emotionally intelligent are you and your team?

Brain chemistry

Our limbic brain controls our feelings and our ability to trust colleagues and clients. Trust is a feeling, not a behaviour, and our limbic brain feeds our body with chemicals to determine whether we trust or distrust a person, helping us to form bonds at an emotional level.

Oxytocin

Oxytocin is the hormone that underlies trust. It is also an antidote to depressive feelings. It is produced when we make physical contact with someone, and is often known as the love hormone. We're not suggesting that you go around falling in love with or hugging your colleagues and clients! We're talking about handshakes, eye contact and demonstrating warmth and compassion to build rapport.

Oxytocin gives us the ability to empathise and be generous. It is also known as the pro-social hormone, as it allows us to build bonds with others. Generosity and empathy must be unconditional. If we carry out an act of generosity, no matter how small, and it has come from a place of doing the right thing rather than following a process, then oxytocin is released in our body and in that of the recipient, and a stronger bond is formed.

The more acts of generosity we show our colleagues and clients, the more meaningful our relationships will be. If we merely follow a process and go through the motions, the interaction will be transactional. We rely on technology to follow processes and be compliant, but we need human interaction to build trust.

When we do business with people we like and trust, more oxytocin is produced in our bodies. This is why it's also called the happiness hormone. Not only do we feel good, the recipient feels good too.

As leaders, we need to empower our teams to do the right thing for clients. Knowing when to bend the rules to help a client will cement the relationship, and the individual and the organisation will gain credibility.

US-based company Zappos is an excellent example of an organisation that has thrown traditional rules out of the window. All employees are empowered to make decisions that maintain the company's legendary customer-service standard. CEO Tony Hsieh links customer experience and employee empowerment directly to profits: 'Happier employees lead to strong, nurturing relationships and a more profitable business.'

Another benefit of oxytocin? It boosts the immune system, leaving us less susceptible to illness. And a healthier workforce ultimately leads to a more profitable business.

While oxytocin is very beneficial, it also has a downside. It is responsible for unconscious bias and favouritism. Individuals considered to be outside of a group are viewed less favourably than those inside a group. We will explore unconscious bias later in this section.

Cortisol

The hormone cortisol can offset all the benefits of oxytocin in our system. While cortisol isn't produced in the brain (it comes from the adrenal glands), it is important to mention the impact cortisol can have on building trusted relationships.

Cortisol inhibits the release of oxytocin, therefore decreasing our ability to be empathetic and show generosity. It also interferes with learning and memory, weakens the immune system and increases aggression.

It is often referred to as the stress hormone, and while it is useful in fight-or-flight situations, it can be damaging if sustained in the body for long periods. If sustained, the risk of depression and mental illness is increased and life expectancy can be lowered.

Cortisol is released when we are stressed out or fearful. Loretta Graziano Breuning, PhD, founder of the Inner Mammal Institute, says, 'Cortisol commands attention when a threat is perceived (internal or external). It creates the feeling that you will die if you don't make it stop. Each cortisol spurt connects neurons that turn on the bad feeling when similar circumstances are met. Disappointment triggers cortisol too.'

Work-related stress has a significant impact on organisational performance. The UK government's Health and Safety Executive reports that the total number of UK working days lost due to work-related stress, depression or anxiety was 11.7 million in 2015/2016. And 37% of all work-related ill-health cases involved stress, depression or anxiety. Although there are significantly higher rates of work-related stress in professional occupations, it affects all occupations and all industries.

Employees in a command-and-control culture will have cortisol permanently activated in their bodies. This is not natural; it should only be present in real fight-or-flight situations. If we are feeling stressed out and have a negative mindset, this of course will negatively affect our behaviour, which in turn will affect our business relationships.

If an organisation's culture is conducive to an increase of oxytocin, rather than cortisol, our employees' ability to form bonds at an emotional level, both internally and externally, will be maximised.

The cost of work-related stress is significant. Companies that don't help their people to manage their mindsets and don't create a positive internal culture will see more employee absences, lower performance and a reduced bottom line.

Optimum stress for performance

It might seem odd, but we do need a certain amount of stress in order to perform at our best. With no stress whatsoever, we would be completely demotivated. To be energised and focused, we need to be in a state of peak stress, the sweet spot for achievement. Too little stress means that we are unengaged, bored and uninspired; too much can lead to burnout or illness. The sweet spot will vary for each of us. The level of stress that one individual may find motivating could leave others either bored or floored. It's a case of testing this out for yourself and being aware of when you start to feel that the stress is too great. With the optimum amount of stress, we are in flow and achieving our personal best.

Unconscious bias

Most of us think we know what we believe in. At a conscious level that may well be true, but at an unconscious level, many of us hold prejudices that we are unaware of. We categorise people by weight, age, gender, and skin colour, as well as by level of education, accent, abilities, social status and job title, amongst other things.

We do this to prevent our brains from processing too much information. And these categorisations can then lead us to take actions based on bias—as we have made assumptions. We can challenge this unintentional discrimination though. The more we expose ourselves to groups of people who are different from our own groups, the less likely we are to feel prejudice against them and the more likely we are to challenge negative stereotypes.

Background, environment, family influences and previous experiences all shape our unconscious thinking.

If we understand how unconscious bias affects our actions and behaviours, we can learn how to reprogramme our thinking. This will enable us to build better relationships.

 Are you aware of the bias in you and your team?

Consequences of unconscious bias

Unconscious bias can:

- affect recruitment decisions
- limit workforce diversity
- hinder teamwork within the organisation
- stifle creativity and innovation
- negatively affect employees' performance
- contribute to low morale
- lead to more resignations and grievance procedures
- damage an organisation's reputation/brand
- cause more complaints to be filed, and
- result in loss of business/revenue.

The benefits of diversity

Diversity can result in:

- improved customer service that meets the needs of clients from different cultural and social backgrounds
- an adaptable workforce that offers differing perspectives when identifying solutions to problems
- a larger pool of candidates to recruit from, and
- business growth (due to an innovative workforce).

Self-reflection

To achieve optimum performance, it's important to manage your mindset. For best results we recommend daily self-reflection, which will solidify good habits and behaviours.

Self-reflection is time dedicated specifically to thinking about how you are managing your mindset and the factors that are leading to poor or excellent performance.

Setting aside time in your day for self-reflection will improve your ability to recognise helpful thoughts, feelings and behaviours, as well as unhelpful ones. Consider your mindset—in what areas is it fixed-based? In what areas is it growth-based? Have you displayed any unconscious bias? Is your mindset more positive or more negative?

Many people spend time reflecting on tangible achievements, on things on their 'to-do' lists, but few of us reflect on how our mindset is performing.

Here's a simple self-reflection exercise. Write a list of adjectives that describe how you felt during the last 24 hours. These could range from excited, focused, elated and joyful to sad, disappointed, anxious, and fearful. Really think about how you have felt and be as specific as possible.

People often use the term 'stressed' to describe any negative emotion, when in fact they might be anxious, worried, overworked or overwhelmed. Our brains like to generalise, but it is much more helpful to be as specific as possible.

After three consecutive days of self-reflection, if you notice a pattern of negativity, see this as a warning that your mindset needs some attention.

How has your mindset performed during the last 24 hours?

In your workbook you will find additional material to help with the self-reflection exercise.
www.firstimpressions.uk.com/trusted/

Priming your mind

Priming the mind means making it ready for an interaction. This is much more than arriving with a checklist; it's also about preparing to be present with the client you are about to meet.

Have you ever decided to buy a new car and suddenly it seems that every second car on the road is the make and model you decided on? Of course, there are no more of these cars on the road than normal. The thing that has changed is your mind! You have primed your mind—your reticular activating system, to be precise—to seek out these cars.

The reticular activating system (RAS) acts as an antenna. It seeks out the things we focus on; hence, we spot more of the car we are looking to buy.

The RAS can help us to seek out the behaviours we want to exhibit when building trusted relationships with our clients. Time spent thinking about the characteristics we want to demonstrate in our interactions will be time well spent. For example, if you wish to show warmth and empathy, you'll want to consider using a softer tone, a lower volume and a lower pitch. You'll also want to slow down your speaking speed, and choose words that convey warmth; i.e., phrases such as 'I understand' or 'How can I support you?'

You can also prime your mind in terms of outcome. Considering the desired outcome of an interaction prior to client meetings will help you to adapt your behaviour (if any challenges come up) while keeping your goal in mind.

During a recent programme with Lloyds Bank, we discussed the concept of priming the mind with Mark Cadwallader and Hannah Alexander, regional director and area director respectively. Mark and Hannah shared the following:

'Before attending a meeting, we always try to get our heads clear by running through the following:

- What are the main goals for the meeting? What do we want to achieve?
- Who will be at the meeting and what type of atmosphere are we trying to create? Relaxed and informal or professional and formal?
- What mindset do we need? Do we need to dial up confidence and assertiveness or dial these down and perhaps dial up humility and openness?

'Getting in the zone before the meeting and doing a pre-play improves the meeting's quality for all.'

Managing your mindset

Mandy Cooper, CEO of Bayberry Clinics, told us, 'In business, when organisations poorly implement change management processes or when communications break down, this can lead to fear, a lack of trust, and higher levels of stress and anxiety. Staff can get locked into something akin to a trance state: introspecting and ruminating on what "might" happen—which for many people is inevitably pessimistic. There is a duality of responsibility here: employers need to understand that silence and miscommunication are the enemies of trust, and staff need to have an awareness of their own catastrophic rumination that is undermining their own well-being. Never was the phrase "it's good to talk" more apt.

'Similarly, when we feel ourselves entering a high-pressure situation—which could be an interview, a meeting, a presentation (and many people will understand the anxiety associated with public speaking)—the anxiety response is at risk of temporarily disabling our access to our "executive function": the bit where we store all those clever things we are going to say to our audience. This leads to stumbling over words, forgotten speeches and post-presentation reflection where everything comes flowing back to us, as our anxiety levels decrease once more. Understanding these responses is key to learning to control them, and techniques can be successfully utilised to overcome such responses. The imagination is a problem-solving tool— rehearsing whatever you need to do is hugely helpful in preparing for the "performance". This, in itself, decreases anxiety as there is greater confidence in the strategy. However, when you're standing outside the door or about to walk on the platform, that familiar spike of anxiety might still strike. The technique here is to communicate with your own body—to tell it all is well. You can't do this cognitively (you don't believe yourself), but you can do it physiologically with a simple breathing technique.

'Called 7-11 breathing, it works on the premise that breathing is used to stimulate the parasympathetic nervous system. This is the system associated with calm—the opposite of the "fight-or-flight" response. The out-breath decreases blood pressure, slows heart rate and lowers emotions. We need more of this out-breath to convince our brains that we are, in fact, calm and that there is no need for the anxiety response, which will hinder performance. The "7-11" refers to the length of the breaths: breathe in for a count of 7, breathe out for a count of 11. A longer out-breath will lower the emotional response almost instantly, and within four or five breaths, a difference should be felt. This technique is useful in myriad situations—it's even helpful with sleep problems.'

Here are some of Mandy's simple tips to help reduce stress and anxiety.

- **Practise 7-11 breathing.** This is simply breathing in for a count of 7 and out for a count of 11. The effects can be felt in just a few breaths (it's not intended to be a permanent breathing state, just a short-term intervention when you're anxious).
- **Promote education in the workplace.** Make it okay to talk about feeling anxious or stressed. Be non-judgemental, be open and have genuine concern for colleagues at all levels of the organisation. An appropriate (and individually relative) level of stress is a good thing—it's a motivator. It becomes a problem when we are overwhelmed with problems that we cannot resolve or change or with circumstances beyond our resources or control; this leads to burnout (which can often manifest as anxiety, panic or a sense of loss of control).
- **Take a proactive approach to mental health.** Offer regular one-to-one coaching or counselling sessions to talk about maintaining a positive mindset.
- **Get enough sleep.** When we are anxious, we may suffer either from insomnia or too much REM sleep (our brain's way of dealing with emotions). If you wake up having slept but still feeling really tired, this could well be the reason. Try allocating a time early in the day to reflect on things that need your attention—and then once that time period is over, put those thoughts aside until the same time the next day. Be disciplined: bedtime is not the time to sort out all your problems!
- **Practise mindfulness.** We will discuss this shortly.
- **Interact and connect on a human level.** Social media and email create the illusion that we are connecting with people. But we need to build rapport with real people to connect with our innate emotional need for community—people with a shared sense of purpose and mutual understanding. It could be as simple as meeting up with a book group, a sports group or friends. Digital media is an accessory to connection, but it cannot replace it.

- **Be prepared for life changes.** Big life events, such as retirement, for instance, can be a key factor in depression if not approached with planning. In the case of retirement, it is vital to be aware that such a significant change in your daily structure and sense of purpose can dramatically impact your well-being unless alternate goals and a sense of meaning are established. Employers can help with transitions such as retirement, redundancy, job change or even periods of extended leave. To maintain your well-being, it's vital to recognise the feelings associated with such change and how they will herald new definitions of 'community', 'meaning', 'purpose' and 'achievement'.

Which of these tips are useful to you and your team?

Well-being and employee benefits in the workplace

Employee well-being is a hot topic of conversation in the business world today. Ultimately, we can measure our well-being by our levels of happiness, health, comfort and safety.

All too often, our work lives and home lives negatively affect our well-being, and in turn, this negatively affects our professional and personal relationships.

We often hear employers talking about the need for well-being initiatives in the workplace, and citing external reasons for the need. Sometimes, though, we need to look within the organisation itself, as workplace culture can contribute to employees' stress or unhappiness.

As leaders, we have a responsibility to ensure that our teams have healthy mindsets. We must facilitate this through a positive culture.

Birmingham Optical Group has introduced many initiatives to promote employee well-being as a result of extensive staff-engagement surveys.

During monthly one-to-one meetings, employees are given the opportunity to provide feedback and share how they are feeling and how things are at home. This helps both employees and employers to identify any early warning signs. A free helpline has been set up with an outside agency and is available for staff—they can speak to someone over the phone or arrange a face-to-face meet-up at any time.

As part of the company's employee benefits package, reduced fees have been negotiated with local gyms to encourage staff to participate in physical activities. Events such as family days, charity cycle rides, running groups and football tournaments have been arranged to support employee well-being while raising money for worthy causes.

Natalie Ormerod, head of HR and quality at Band Hatton Button Solicitors, sees employee well-being as a priority in her role. She says, 'Probably the most significant well-being initiatives are the introduction of a 'duvet day' for birthdays and fruit being delivered twice a week. We also have a high-quality coffee machine in the kitchen to encourage our employees to take breaks from their desks and increase team bonding. We celebrate long-service awards; arrange a summer and Christmas event for team members and families. There are also regular treats throughout the year, like an egg at Easter, Christmas goodies, and the ice-cream van comes during the summer to keep everyone cool!'

What well-being initiatives and employee benefits could you introduce in your organisation?

Overcoming mindset barriers

There are many ways to overcome mindset barriers. We use the following techniques regularly with clients, and they deliver excellent results.

- Anchoring—has a piece of music ever suddenly transported you to a memorable positive time? Music can take you back to a feeling you once had. It's an external trigger, and your feeling is an internal response that was captured at the time. We can use this same technique, known as anchoring, to help us change our mindset at any given time. It can boost energy, confidence, motivation or any other powerful state. Wearing certain clothing can be an anchor—your lucky jacket, for example. In sport, we also see anchoring rituals. When former English rugby player Jonny Wilkinson prepared to kick, he always carried out the same ritual. In this way, he linked himself to a positive mindset that allowed him to access the most resourceful state for success. To create an anchor, follow these steps.
  ◊ Decide on the positive emotion you wish to anchor (e.g., confidence).
  ◊ Choose a physical anchor to trigger the positive emotion (e.g., squeeze your thumb and forefinger together).
  ◊ Recall a time when you experienced the positive emotion (or imagine a scenario).
  ◊ Activate the anchor when you can feel the emotion at its peak state (most intense).
  ◊ When the experience begins to fade, release the physical anchor and distract yourself from your current state (you may want to count down from ten to zero).
  ◊ Repeat these steps several times to make the memory more vivid each time.
  ◊ Apply the anchor and check that the desired emotional state occurs.

◊ Test it by thinking of a situation where you may need to use this anchor; see if it's effective.

- Modified language and visualisation—the statements we use to describe ourselves are powerful. Do you ever notice yourself saying 'I can't' or 'I'm not' statements? For example, 'I'm not confident enough to do this'. This statement limits capabilities and straight away disempowers you. In this state, it is difficult to access positive emotions; the limiting belief takes over, and even if it is not true, in that moment, you believe it is. To overcome limiting beliefs and prevent self-sabotage, try the following techniques.
  ◊ Notice your language, both the language you speak out loud and the language you use in your head, known as self-talk. Any time you make a blanket statement about yourself, or catch yourself thinking that you can't do something, take some quiet time and note any self-limiting beliefs.
  ◊ Get into the habit of modifying your language; for example, if you have written 'I am not confident', change it to 'I am working towards having more confidence'. It's a subtle shift but a powerful one.
  ◊ Pick a date in the future when you want to be more confident and regularly spend time visualising how you want that confidence to manifest.
  ◊ Visualise your desired outcome often, with as much clarity as you possibly can.

- Positive self-talk—practise the art of positive self-talk. Tailor it to the goal you are trying to achieve. For example, as you enter a room at a networking event, you might repeat instructions to yourself: 'Shoulders back, head upright, good posture'. Or it could be a phrase to motivate you: 'I can do this' or 'I've got it handled'.

- Power posing—we have written about this in the *Communication* section, as the technique covers body language as well as mindset. According to Amy Cuddy, professor of psychology at Harvard University, 'Our bodies change our minds, and our minds can change our behaviour, our behaviour can change our outcomes'.

- Self-awareness and feedback—very often we are unaware of the mindset barriers we create for ourselves, but others can spot them. Create an environment and culture that encourages feedback and challenges employees constructively. We don't always know what we don't know!

- Coaching or mentoring—a great coach or mentor can really help expand your mindset and push your thinking.

- Modelling—Richard Bandler, co-founder of Neuro-Linguistic Programming (NLP), says, 'We take the very best of what people do, synthesise it down, make it learnable and share it with each other—that is…NLP'. Why reinvent the wheel when we can learn from someone who has already mastered the skill or behaviour that we are trying to learn? If we understand the beliefs, physiology and specific thought processes that underlie a skill or behaviour, we can replicate it.

- Reframing—by putting a positive twist on something, we can change the way we think and feel about it. For example, say you receive news from a client: the timescale for a project has been drastically reduced because the current software will be unsupported earlier than planned. You might be inclined to think your organisation can't meet the challenge. Here's a simple reframe: 'We have a big challenge ahead of us, and we are up to the challenge. We can do this!'

Andrew Haworth, managing director of Bartle Hall Hotel, Lancashire, says, 'People's emotional well-being can fluctuate, and it's helping people to understand that this is normal. For me, mindset is everything. If our employee is not confident, they will be sabotaging themselves through thinking they are not good enough. Whether it is someone who has worked here for a week or 20 years, helping them with mindset is paramount.'

Mindfulness

Donna's story   I didn't hear the term 'mindfulness' until September 2003. I was excited to be starting a new phase of my life—I was returning to work after a four-year career break following the birth of my son, who was born with cerebral palsy.

'Returning to work' is probably the wrong phrase to use, as I've never worked so hard as I did during those years. My son's disability was the pathway to securing my new position as an associate director on the trust board of an NHS Mental Health and Children's Trust. As is usual with NHS appointments, there was an extensive induction program to work through.

I soon realised that this was no run-of-the-mill induction. The third day was dedicated to my well-being as an employee, and included a meeting with the hospital chaplain, a one-to-one with the HR director and a workshop introducing me to 'mindfulness'.

What is mindfulness?

Professor Mark Williams, former director of the Oxford Mindfulness Centre, says that mindfulness means knowing what is going on inside and outside ourselves, moment by moment.

'It's easy to stop noticing the world around us. It's also easy to lose touch with the way our bodies are feeling and to end up living "in our heads"—caught up in our thoughts without stopping to notice how those thoughts are driving our emotions and behaviour,' he says.

'An important part of mindfulness is reconnecting with our bodies and the sensations they experience. This means waking up to the sights, sounds, smells and tastes of the present moment. That might be something as simple as the feel of a banister as we walk upstairs.'

How can mindfulness benefit us?

Becoming aware of the present moment can help us enjoy the world around us more and understand ourselves better.

Professor Williams also says, 'This lets us stand back from our thoughts and start to see their patterns. Gradually, we can train ourselves to notice when our thoughts are taking over and realise that thoughts are simply "mental events" that do not have to control us.

'Awareness of this kind also helps us notice signs of stress or anxiety earlier and helps us deal with them better.'

Steps I (Donna) take to make mindfulness a habit

- I walk daily at 6 am and observe nature around me.
- I drink eight glasses of water mindfully each day. This involves paying attention to the feeling of the glass in my hand, the act of breathing, the drinking of the water, the sensation of the water in my mouth and the swallowing of the water. All I am thinking about at this time is the act of drinking.
- I pay attention to my breathing at various points throughout the day. When I am aware of my in-breath and out-breath, my breathing calms, and this in turn calms my mind.

All of these activities allow me to connect with the current moment so I can be present with a clear mind and focus on the here and now.

Build a mindfulness habit

Pick a regular time—for example, the morning journey to work or a walk at lunchtime—during which you dedicate yourself to being aware of the sensations created by the world around you.

Try something new

Trying new things, such as sitting in a different seat during meetings or going somewhere new for lunch, can also help you notice the world in a new way.

Some people find that doing gentle yoga or walking helps them to cope with an overly busy mind.

Caroline Suggett, executive coach and mindfulness teacher, tells us:

'Thoughts are not facts—thoughts are just thoughts. They are not reality. Things you may worry about or imagine happening will probably never happen. Imagine thoughts as just clouds passing by. Your mind is the clear, steady blue sky. Noticing that you are separate to your thoughts means the thoughts lose their emotional power over you. This creates a pause for you to notice you can choose to focus on what IS actually happening in each moment'.

How could you introduce mindfulness into your daily routine?

Mastering the art of managing your mindset is a key component of building trust. Getting it wrong can really damage your credibility; getting it right can take you one step closer to finding your T-Spot.

Credibility sleuth

 Credibility thief

- Cultivate a growth mindset through hard work, mentoring and perseverance, as this will enable development.

- Consider the importance of a high level of emotional intelligence. It allows us to handle relationships judiciously and empathetically.

- Find ways to maximise oxytocin production. Oxytocin helps us to build maximum trust, to empathise and to be generous.

- Bring your unconscious bias into your conscious awareness to reprogramme your thinking.

- Set aside dedicated self-reflection time to help manage your mindset and catch any dips before they spiral out of control.

- Prime your mind for all interactions to give you the best chance of success.

- Build strategies to proactively manage your mindset in high-pressure situations.

- Support healthy mindsets in employees through a positive culture that encourages well-being initiatives, such as mindfulness.

- Learn techniques to overcome mindset barriers.

- A fixed mindset in any situation can be very damaging to your credibility.

- Low emotional intelligence equates to having difficulty reading and controlling emotions.

- The stress hormone cortisol can block oxytocin's benefits. Find ways to achieve optimum 'stress' for performance.

- Left unchecked, your judgement of others will narrow your world.

- An unhealthy amount of negative thinking over a prolonged period of time can affect your emotional well-being.

- If you are not priming your mind, you are not bringing your best characteristics to your interactions.

- A reactive approach to your mental health could escalate stress and anxiety.

- Toxic cultures can contribute significantly to employees' stress and unhappiness.

- Without a toolbox of strategies, a healthy mindset is left to chance.

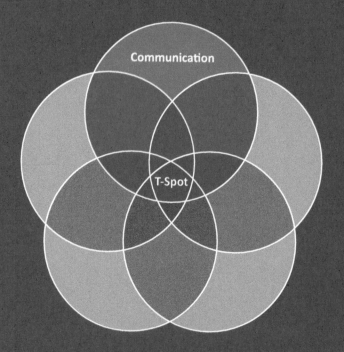

Communication

T-Spot

'The effectiveness of communication is not defined by the communication, but by the response.'

— Milton Erickson, psychiatrist and psychologist

Communication is at the heart of every organisation. As our world becomes increasingly digital, we need to hone our communication skills. Communication is multifaceted: verbal, non-verbal, visual and written. To ensure information is meaningful for the listener, it's imperative that we choose the form that suits the context, situation and environment. Listening effectively and knowing when to pause so the other person can speak are also great communication skills to master.

Communication

When relationships break down, a breakdown in communication is often the cause.

Let's start at the beginning—how to communicate when we first meet someone.

What is rapport?

Rapport is a state of harmonious understanding that enables better communication between individuals or groups. Rapport happens on an unconscious level, and it is a fundamental way to build trust and confidence in a relationship. It helps people to feel as though they are in sync or on the same wavelength. When we hit it off with someone, rapport happens naturally, but rapport-building skills can also be developed. We shouldn't underestimate the amount of effort needed to build great relationships.

Techniques to help build rapport

- Seek to understand the other person's point of view, rather than expect the other person to understand you first. You don't have to like or agree with this point of view.
- Take a genuine interest in learning what is important to the other person.
- Ask open questions.
- Respect the other person's time and energy.
- Adopt a similar stance to the other person in terms of body language, tone of voice, gestures and speed of speaking. This is known as matching and mirroring, and it will help you get in sync with each other—don't do it too overtly though, or it will turn into a game of Simon Says!
- Pick up on key words and phrases the other person uses and subtly build them into the conversation.
- Remember the basics of body language: handshaking, eye contact, smiling, good posture and sincerity. More on this shortly.
- Use non-threatening topics for small talk.
- Show empathy.

Small talk or deeper connection

Psychologist Matthias Mehl found that deeper connection always makes people happier. 'By engaging in meaningful conversations, we manage to impose meaning on an otherwise pretty chaotic world.'

In a study he conducted, the happiest people reported that they experienced twice as many substantive conversations as conversations based on small talk.

Hello, my name is...

Building rapport is so important, and it's also quite simple with a little focus and attention. In fact, it's so simple it's often overlooked. It helps put us at ease, and affects how the other person responds to us. Even if we are highly skilled and qualified in our fields, we cannot skip the rapport-building phase during any interaction. In order to influence and persuade others, we have to have built rapport first.

Dr Kate Granger founded the #hellomynameis campaign to remind healthcare professionals of the importance of introductions. She believed in going back to basics, and that an introduction runs much deeper than common courtesy. For Dr Granger, an introduction is about human beings making a connection.

'One of the first things taught in medical school is that when you approach a patient, you say your name, your role and what you are going to do,' she said. It was only when she was admitted to hospital herself, after being diagnosed with terminal cancer, that Dr Granger realised this standard was rarely being met. She observed that many doctors didn't introduce themselves or make eye contact, leaving her feeling insignificant. '[When people introduced themselves] it really did make a difference to how comfortable I was and less lonely I was in hospital.'

She said that the doctor who delivered the news that her cancer had spread did not introduce himself or look her in the eye. She told BBC Radio 4's *Today* programme that 'the lack of introductions really made [her] feel like just a diseased body and not a real person'.

The #hellomynameis campaign has the backing of over 400,000 NHS staff. It has also caught the attention of high-profile celebrities and politicians. Well done, Dr Kate, for bringing this to the attention of the masses and taking action. Very sadly, Dr Kate Granger passed away in 2016, but her legacy will continue as her husband now champions her cause.

You may be incredulous when we say that basic communication skills are not being carried out, but in fact, service companies in all types of industries engage us to help their employees improve their people skills.

An NHS trust we worked with was really on board with this idea, and is ensuring that all staff are informed of the importance of creating rapport with their patients and are developing their people skills. Though the clinical skills are of course vital, bedside manner is also a crucial part of being an effective clinician.

Do you and your team take time to build rapport with your prospects and clients before moving on to business?

Body language

Body language is a huge topic, so we are going to focus on a few key aspects of it, specifically in regards to building professional relationships. Our body language is an excellent indication of what's going on inside us, so we need to be conscious of what it's saying—otherwise, we can give the game away without meaning to!

Verbal communication began around 100,000 years ago. Before that, we relied on non-verbal communication. We therefore all have the ability to read these non-verbal signals, as it is instinctive.

Alex (Sandy) Pentland, director of the Human Dynamics Lab at the Massachusetts Institute of Technology, has researched the signals we send out through our non-verbals. Using sociometric monitors, he found that he could predict the outcomes of business negotiations and pitches, as well as which clinicians might face litigation. These predictions were based solely on analyses of face-to-face interactions and unconscious signalling. No verbal communication was analysed in this research, which was carried out over five decades.

The monitors are small, wearable computers that detect all movement, including facial expressions and body language.

Greeting

The greeting is your first opportunity to create a good impression. It consists of several body language cues that all happen simultaneously:

◊ Eye contact – maintain a steady gaze (don't stare!) for around 70% of the time.
◊ Smiling – a smile shows warmth and friendliness.

◊ Handshaking – a firm handshake is important. The palm must face inwards as a sign of equality. The grip should be firm, not too strong or too weak. Keep your left arm by your side. In the UK, we tend to do two or three shakes. If it lasts too long, it can be uncomfortable. Handshaking is often seen as basic, but we've found it's one of the key aspects of the greeting that can leave a poor impression. Mastering this skill is simple and impactful, since touch is the most powerful and effective non-verbal cue. We will cover more on this topic shortly, as our clients often want to discuss it.

◊ Posture – keep your shoulders back, no slouching, especially when walking into a room or on a stage.

◊ Head position – keeping your head in an upright position conveys confidence. A lowered head can signal a lack in confidence and a raised head can signal arrogance.

◊ Gestures – keep body language open, e.g., no folded arms or legs.

As well, watch out for negative body language, particularly if you are feeling anxious (as this will show); e.g., rubbing hands together, tapping feet, playing with jewellery or hair. In displaying these behaviours, you immediately rob yourself of credibility.

Facial expressions

Facial expressions are a major component of non-verbal communication and can effectively demonstrate your involvement in a conversation. A stoic, unmoving face will seem impersonal and robotic, so remain as tuned-in as possible without appearing cartoonish. Smile as often as the conversation allows, raise eyebrows to illustrate interest and express seriousness when the time calls for it.

American psychologist Dr Paul Ekman has been studying facial and micro-expressions for over 50 years. His work demonstrates that most of us have the ability to identify seven universal emotions: anger, fear, sadness, disgust, surprise, contempt and happiness.

His findings show that many of us are able to identify how a person is feeling by reading his or her facial expressions. We intuitively search for clues in the positioning of the eyes, nose and mouth. Recognition of the seven core emotions is instinctive, and is done unconsciously. We can also do this consciously, which helps us to build rapport. Each emotion has its own unique signal or facial-expression clue. Our facial expressions come from an area of the brain that we don't have control over—they are an automatic response.

According to Dr Ekman, micro-expressions are those that occur within 1/25th of a second and expose a person's true emotions. These facial expressions are the same on every man, woman or child, regardless of cultural background, and 95% of the population cannot inhibit them; there is some 'leakage' through small, involuntary cues. We can hone our skills to improve how we read micro-expressions. Ekman's research also shows that people who are skilled at reading micro-expressions are better liked by co-workers.

He says, 'When you can recognise the expressions of others you become more sensitive to their real feelings. Improving your ability to recognise others' emotions increases your connections with other people and will enhance your relationships.'

When you want to really engage with people, observe the degree to which they are showing expressions through the face and match this through your own expressions. Often when we have good rapport with someone this happens naturally. Our facial gestures can also betray us in many ways, so we must be aware of how others see us.

Clearly we don't often see ourselves when we are communicating, so asking for feedback is a useful development tool.

Handshake

When working with senior-level managers, we would start the session with a brief icebreaker exercise. The amount of discussion it provoked proved very interesting. The exercise was simply to shake hands. It's a brief gesture, and a standard introduction in business. It's something we do all the time. But have you ever stopped to consider what your handshake is saying about you?

It's important to add that cultural differences need to be considered. We are talking primarily about shaking hands in the Western World. We will cover cultural differences separately.

Story from Lyn I've always believed that someone's handshake is an indication of his or her personality, an instinct I honed early in my career. When working as a project manager, I would consciously observe the greetings my clients gave me when meeting them for the first time.

A limp handshake would instantly put me on guard. It was often an indication of someone who was less assertive, often less effective, and I would know that I needed to monitor his or her work more closely to ensure that the project was delivered on time. Equally, if I received a 'bone-crusher' handshake, I would surmise that the individual was a dominant character and I would have to carefully manage his or her more assertive approach throughout the project.

In all of my time working in professional services, around 20 years in total, the handshake test has rarely let me down. It's always been a remarkably accurate indicator of the type of person I'm working with.

Research carried out by William F. Chaplin et al. (2000) investigated the link between handshake and personality. It revealed that handshaking characteristics are related to both personality and the impressions people form about each other. During the study, subjects shook hands several times with a number of researchers. The researchers reported that the handshake of each subject was the same each time. This shows that a person's handshake will remain the same unless he or she is taught otherwise.

Research by Florin Dolcos (2012) shows that strangers form better impressions about those who proffer a hand, as this demonstrates confidence. It also shows that these people are perceived as more trustworthy and more competent. Most interestingly, the research found that people are more interested in doing business with someone who initiates a handshake.

Handshakes originated as a traditional greeting in the days where people carried swords. Offering the right hand for a handshake proved that you came in peace and were not holding a weapon. It was also a sign of trust, showing that you believed the other person was not going to take out his or her sword to harm you.

So how do you get it right and convey that you're confident and competent in such a brief gesture? To make the right impression, a firm handshake is important; the grip should be neither too strong nor too weak. There should also be good eye contact, positive body language and an equal balance of power.

Trying to select an image of a handshake for this book was challenging, and this reinforced to us how much ambiguity surrounds the gesture. Many of the images we found showed an imbalance of power, particularly between men and women. So we decided, after much searching, to photograph our own!

Our image shows a good handshake with all the attributes mentioned above.

We had fun being photographed, and demonstrating some of the poor handshakes we've heard stories about: the bone-crusher handshake, the wet-fish handshake, the subservient handshake, the dominant handshake and the 'I'm not really interested in talking to you' handshake!

In your workbook you will find photographs of these handshakes. We're sure you have experienced some of them too!
www.firstimpressions.uk.com/trusted/

We are often asked whether women should shake hands, and if handshake styles should be different for men and women. We strongly believe that a firm handshake, accompanied by a smile and good eye contact, is a must for both genders as it will help to convey trust and competence.

Do you pass the handshake test? If you're unsure, test it out on a colleague and ask for feedback.

Meeting and greeting: Getting it right across cultures

Today, as we experience change like never before, all eyes are firmly focused on world leaders. Everything they say comes under intense scrutiny, and while their words and promises may change—and often do—a clear indicator of their composure, poise and confidence in any situation is their body language, in particular their greetings.

On an international stage, there is absolutely no room for error. One error in judgement may be seen as clumsy at best and insulting or disrespectful at worst.

It may feel like the eyes of the world are on you when you're meeting and greeting clients and colleagues. You're representing your company and you want to get it right; plus, your colleagues are looking to you for guidance. You may feel the pressure to maintain your professional reputation, as well as the pressure to make a great impression.

Our tips for getting it right across cultures

- **Do your research.** There is a lot of information online, and some sources are more credible than others. Make sure you're referring to a reliable source, and make sure it's current.

- **Check your calendar.** Understanding cultures and customs is a good place to start, but you must also make sure you're aware of particular events and religious occasions. These would be particularly important to know in the hospitality industry, for example.

- **Politely enquire.** Ask your colleagues about their previous experiences of welcoming clients to your organisation, and about their interactions with these clients elsewhere. Determine what worked well and if there is anything they would do differently.

- **Wait and see.** If you're really unsure about how to act, allow the person you're meeting to initiate the greeting. While this may not be an appropriate long-term strategy to set you apart as a confident leader, it will allow you to show the utmost respect for getting it right. Michelle Obama demonstrated a great example of this when she met King Salman bin Abdulaziz, the new king of Saudi Arabia, and his dignitaries. Aware of the strong Islamic rules about men meeting women other than family members, she patiently waited to see how each man reacted. If a hand was offered, she shook it and smiled; if not, she simply smiled and nodded. She showed great respect for their culture and played it just right.

- **Invest.** Investing in your professional skills will pay dividends throughout your entire career. While emails and phone calls might be an efficient way to communicate, the importance of the face-to-face meeting serves as a true opportunity to build a more personal connection.

The art of listening

'Most people do not listen with the intent to understand; they listen with the intent to reply.' – *Stephen R. Covey, educator and author*

Focused listening is one of the most important business skills to master. We need to listen for a variety of reasons: to understand, to learn, to obtain necessary facts and information and sometimes purely to enjoy.

A high level of self-awareness in this area is paramount to building trusted relationships. In today's highly digitised world, where devices bleep, ring and vibrate all around us, our attention can be pulled in many directions. When communicating we need to actively listen and remain present and focused on the person in front of us.

A story from Donna When attending networking events, I'm always fascinated when observing people around the room. At a recent networking function, I was very aware of some attendees clearly struggling with the art of active listening. At these events, people are often so preoccupied with looking around the room to target their next prospect that they don't engage with the person they are standing in front of. This results in wasted opportunities.

Active listening is paying close attention. It is absorbing what is being communicated not only through words but also through emotion, body language and facial expressions.

To show that you are truly listening, do the following:

- nod
- lean towards the other person
- smile (where appropriate)
- maintain an open posture
- give positive reinforcement
- ask questions to further your understanding
- defer judgement, and
- allow the speaker to finish his or her point before giving your own opinions.

Gestures

'They are not approachable—they have their arms folded.'
If we were paid every time we heard someone say this, we
would be very rich by now! Folded arms in themselves don't
indicate being defensive. It's important to note that body
language is an entire language, not just a single gesture
in isolation. If someone with folded arms is also wearing
a scowl, then it is likely he or she is being defensive,
but people often fold their arms because they are cold,
need reassurance or are just comfortable in that position.
However, it's useful to know that many people equate
folded arms with defensive, so bear that in mind if you don't
want to send out this message.

Show of hands

Your hands are a big part of your conversation. Whether you
point, steeple your hands together or put your hands behind
your back, every gesture adds to your communication. It
is therefore useful to know what these gestures mean so
you're aware of the messages you're sending out. You
could be consistently communicating something that is
counter to what you intend. An awareness of your gestures
can help you to identify and correct any negative ones. Here
are the most common gestures we see in business:

- **Pointing.** Done with a smile, this is not a bad thing; it can
serve to emphasise your message. Pointing and frowning,
on the other hand, will be seen as negative and aggressive.
- **Steepling fingertips.** This shows power and confidence.
Avoid doing this when you want to be persuasive, as it can
sometimes be read as arrogance.
- **Holding hands behind back.** This also displays
confidence, as it leaves the front of the torso exposed. The
gesture is often used by people in authority.

- **Placing palms up or down.** Open palms signal openness and inclusion; hidden palms communicate the opposite. Downward-facing palms show dominance and defiance. If a person has downward-facing palms when negotiating, you are unlikely to move him or her.
- **Chopping.** (Imagine the hand as an axe striking a piece of wood.) Again, this often demonstrates defiance. It can be used to make a point. Just be careful that the rest of your body language is not too aggressive.
- **Rubbing palms together.** This signals positive expectation.
- **Putting hands on hips.** Though this can communicate dominance, it can also demonstrate readiness.
- **Wringing hands.** This is usually a sign of nervous anticipation or anxiety.
- **Placing hands on face.** Generally this is seen as a sign of insecurity, while touching the mouth can be a sign of dishonesty. Chin stroking or resting your chin on your hand is a sign of thoughtful decision-making or reflection.

We also need to be aware of gesticulation when speaking. Some people are very expressive and wave their hands around wildly, while others are more self-contained with their gestures. There isn't one method that is better than another—it will depend on the situation, the message and the recipient. Consciously use gestures that will help you to get your message across, rather than hinder your communication. The way people use their hands can give you clues as to how they wish to communicate. We will cover this later in this section.

Space invaders

Each of us has an arm's-length region around the body that is considered our personal space. If people encroach on that space, we might feel quite uncomfortable or threatened. While social interactions with people we know well are different, generally in business, a good distance is an arm's length.

Posture power

 It is important to consider posture when sitting and standing. Sitting and standing tall with your shoulders back is a sign of confidence, while slouching can make you look sloppy and/or bored.

As Amy Cuddy found in her research, posture can have a significant effect on mindset, too. 'Our bodies change our minds, and our minds can change our behaviour. Our behaviour can change our outcomes. Our non-verbals govern how others think and feel about us.' She asked students to hold what she calls 'power poses' for two minutes. They were given either high- or low-power poses to emulate. High-power poses included the 'Wonder Woman' (hands on hips) and 'pride' (arms in the air).

Readings of the students' cortisol and testosterone levels were taken before and after each power pose. Results showed that high-power poses reduced cortisol (stress hormone) by up to 25% and increased testosterone (power hormone) by as much as 20%. The students' risk tolerance was also higher after they adopted high-power poses; those who'd adopted low-power poses were more risk adverse. The candidates adopting low-power poses experienced a 10% decrease in testosterone and a 15% increase in cortisol. In real terms, you can increase your confidence, assertiveness and comfort level by adopting high-power poses for two minutes.

You may wish to adopt these poses prior to going into a situation that would normally cause you to feel anxious or low in confidence. We'd love to hear your stories on how this helps you.

See Amy Cuddy's TED Talk for further information on power poses: www.ted.com/talks/amy_cuddy_your_body_language_shapes_who_you_are

Lyn's story I used this technique with a client who got nervous when delivering presentations to more senior people in his organisation. Before his next presentation, he adopted a power pose in his office. He reported increased confidence levels and was able to deliver his presentation without any fear.

Hannah's story 'When Donna and Lyn came to present to a small group of talented colleagues, I knew it would be good but I didn't envisage that they would give us a tip that would not only make a difference to the group but to the wider team. The tip I'm talking about is the power pose. Lyn and Donna explained the science and physiology behind the power pose and got the group to have a go. The positive change in the energy and confidence was instant and remarkable.

'Since that event I have shared the power pose with numerous colleagues, male and female, in various job roles and encourage them to incorporate this into their daily routine. They can use it particularly when they may be facing a challenging situation. My team members always adopt a power pose at the start of our team meetings to help us increase the energy levels. I have been blown away by the feedback, colleagues telling me stories about how they did a quick power pose in the loo before a job interview, a power pose in the car before a difficult meeting and my favourite, a power pose before a first date! Each interaction went better than they had first anticipated as they felt extra confident and that confidence shone through. I know that Lyn and Donna didn't invent the power pose but I thank them for introducing me to it.' Hannah Alexander is an area director of SME banking, Lloyds Banking Group

Happy feet

Feet can be a real giveaway when it comes to how we are truly feeling. Because feet are the furthest body part from the brain, we have less awareness of what we are doing with them. We often have more control over what our face is doing than our feet. Lower-body movements increase significantly when people are lying.

Consider the following:

- **Tapping.** According to psychologist Paul Ekman, this increases if someone is feeling frustrated, uncomfortable or lying.

- **Positioning.** Next time you are networking, take a look at the foot position of the person you are talking to. If the feet are pointing away from you, they want to beat a hasty retreat! In a group conversation, people will point their feet towards the people they are most interested in engaging with.

- **Tucking away.** Crossed ankles and feet pushed back under a chair demonstrate that the person is not engaged in the conversation. People involved in a conversation put their feet into it.

If you catch yourself adopting any negative poses with your feet, shift your physiology and you will notice a shift in your mindset.

The eyes have it

We have already talked about eye contact in greetings. But the eyes are such an important feature in communication we wanted to delve a little deeper.

Aim to hold eye contact around 70% of the time during a business interaction (while listening). Holding eye contact continually would be strange. When speaking, we tend to shift our gaze away while thinking about what we want to say, and this is fine.

Raised eyebrows can show surprise or submission. We can also use this gesture to say hello to someone we know or like without speaking. Lowered eyebrows clearly signal dominance and aggression.

Our Neuro-Linguistic Programming (NLP) studies have revealed that eye movements can give us clues about how people are processing information. They help us determine whether people are thinking of something they heard (auditory), something they saw (visual) or something they felt (kinaesthetic), or if they are talking to themselves (audio digital). When eyes move upwards, the person is remembering something visually. If the person is recalling something heard, she will look sideward and the head will tilt. When a person is mentally talking to himself, he will look down and right (as we are looking at him). Looking down and left means the person is connecting with feelings.

Knowing this information, we can use phrases that will connect us to the person we are communicating with.

Auditory: How does that sound? Does that sound good to you?

Visual: How does that look? Can you see how that would work?

Audio digital: Does that make sense? We'll organise the documents for you.

Kinaesthetic: How do you feel about that? How would you like to handle that?

Body language: Final thoughts

Be aware that any time you read body language, it is important to calibrate how a person usually acts. This will help you spot when there is a change in behaviour, which will help you decipher what the person is thinking.

In our experience, many people seem to know a little about body language. They may have received prior training on it and have an academic awareness of the topic, but we don't often see people applying what they know. Rather, they appear to pay lip service to it. Often people remember single gestures but do not read the overall language; therefore, they can totally misread situations. This leads to poor communication and weak relationships.

Body language is powerful and should be taken seriously. Most people could significantly improve their body language, for it is a complex language. Just like a spoken word, a single gesture can have many different meanings. To understand the overall meaning, you must observe the whole picture in context. For example, hands on hips could be a sign of aggression, or the person could just be stretching or being playful. Look at facial expressions and consider tone of voice to help decipher body language meaning.

When using body language in your communication, ensure that it is congruent with the message you are aiming to deliver; this will strengthen your communication. It will also enable you to meet your audience's communication preferences. They will hear the words you are saying and see the body language that goes with them; therefore, they can connect with you through their auditory and visual preferences.

Are you aware of any body language or gestures that could enhance or sabotage relationship building?

Verbal communication

Choose words carefully

The words you use affect the way you are perceived. Generally, effective communicators choose simple, easily understood words and phrases. We recommend that you:

- avoid ambiguity, metaphors and jargon—not everyone will interpret phrases the same way
- ensure that the words are relevant and, of course, not offensive—to anyone
- use proactive or positive words to make a greater impact (words such as 'can', 'will', 'happy' or 'opportunity' rather than 'can't', 'won't', 'difficult' or problem)
- use 'however' rather than 'but', or better still, use 'and'— it is more inclusive and maintains rapport; 'but' and 'however' can sometimes break rapport, as they indicate disagreement
- avoid negatives such as 'don't' and 'can't'; e.g., instead of 'don't panic!' use 'keep calm' (also, consider just what message you are sending with 'don't hesitate to contact me'), and
- be aware of slang, 'text speak' or 'youth speak'—consider its appropriateness in terms of your audience.

Show interest

To demonstrate interest in what is being said, use a style of language similar to the other person's. Using the other person's key words in your response is a good technique, as it shows you have listened and indicates that you are in tune with him or her. Notice the person's pace and tone and try to match it—matching is similar to mirroring (used in body language). It will assist with building rapport.

Use your voice effectively

Unless they have been trained for a specialist role, most people do not give much thought to their voice or how they use it. In fact, many people hardly ever hear their own voice. But we are all aware that we can use our voice to create different effects and convey different messages.

The elements you can vary

Volume: Adjusting the volume of your voice can alert the listener to the nuances of your message.

Pitch: Lowering your pitch at the end of a statement will give your words credibility, whereas raising it will suggest you are unsure of what you are saying. Questions should end on a high note; affirmatives should end on a low note.

Rhythm and pace: Rhythm is the pattern of sound you produce and pace is the speed at which you speak. Speed up the pace when you want to convey humour or excitement, and slow it down when you want to give the listener time to absorb a complex idea.

Timbre (tonality): Timbre represents the character of your voice and the emotion that you are delivering. Match the emotion in your voice to the story you are telling—aligning the words and phrases with voice quality will strengthen your delivery and produce a congruent message. If delivering bad news or showing empathy, use a soft tone. If the message is upbeat and fun, match it with an upbeat, fun tone.

Enunciation and articulation: Clearly and distinctly pronounce your words so others can understand you; avoid mumbling.

Accent and dialect: Society is diverse. You need to be aware of how your accent and regional dialect can be understood or misunderstood. If you know that you have a strong accent, it is important to slow down your speech so that the person you are communicating with can understand you; otherwise the message can easily be lost.

Ⅱ Have you ever received feedback on your voice?

'With the UK being a multicultural society, the ability to communicate well requires greater skill than ever before. It doesn't matter whether you are on the factory floor, in a call centre, customer facing or managing a team—an understanding of how your voice impacts on your communication can make a huge difference to your effectiveness.'
– Priscilla Morris, voice coach

You may wish to consider working with a voice coach to gain an understanding of your voice and the impact it is making.

Consider the message you wish to convey

- Confidence and competence is generally conveyed by a calm, firm and empathetic style of voice—not too quick and not too slow!
- Enthusiasm is generally conveyed by a quicker pace, a higher pitch and more inflection.
- Aggression is usually conveyed through greater volume and a higher pitch.
- Unhappiness or lack of confidence is often associated with a low pitch, slow pace and lack of volume.

Communication styles

We all have a preferred style when it comes to communicating—a style that comes naturally. An understanding of other styles will help you communicate effectively with different types of people.

Organisations around the world use various communication assessment tools, including Myers-Briggs and Insights, depending on their needs and desired outcomes. We use DiSC—we find it very effective, and it provides great results for our clients. And our clients find it easy to understand and remember, so it keeps adding value to their business.

Enhance your knowledge of communication styles

This knowledge will help you:

◊ increase your self-knowledge (i.e., gain an understanding of how you respond to conflict, what motivates you, what causes you stress, how you solve problems)
◊ develop stronger relationship skills (you will be able to identify and respond to your prospects' and clients' communication styles)
◊ improve teamwork in your organisation (you will understand more about your own preferences and those of your colleagues)
◊ minimise conflict and assist in conflict resolution
◊ understand the behavioural strengths in yourself and others
◊ develop your leadership, coaching and mentoring skills
◊ manage others more effectively (you will learn what motivates your team members)
◊ appreciate personal diversity
◊ develop a common language for team discussions, and
◊ make more informed recruitment decisions.

Understanding communication differences

Where would you position yourself on each continuum?

Attitude towards risk: You may be naturally daring and want to rush ahead, with a high tolerance to risk, or you may be more careful and prefer to take things slowly, with a lower tolerance to risk.

Daring   ◄———————►   Careful

Evaluation of ideas/situations: You may be receptive to new ideas, focusing on advantages, or you may be more questioning and sceptical, focusing on disadvantages.

Sceptical   ◄———————►   Accepting

Level of privacy: You may prefer working in a social or collaborative environment, or you may prefer to immerse yourself in solitary tasks.

Outgoing   ◄———————►   Private

Level of pace: You may naturally be driven to set aggressive timescales, or you may prefer more lead time.

Patient   ◄———————►   Driven

Level of diplomacy: You may be frank and speak your mind, or you may be more tactful to avoid offending others.

Tactful   ◄———————►   Frank

Temperament: You may be persistent, perhaps even stubborn, holding firmly to your ideas, or you may be more adaptable and accommodating.

Accommodating   ◄———————►   Strong-willed

Granularity of information: You may prefer high-level information, or you may prefer to dot every *i* and cross every *t*.

Big picture  Detail

Understanding your preferences is a useful start. Now think about someone with whom you have difficulty communicating.

Where would you position this person on each continuum?

Does this give you any insight into where the communication difficulties may lie?

Could you adjust your communication style to improve the interaction?

For example, perhaps you need only the big picture to get on board with an idea, but the person you are communicating with needs detail to feel comfortable making a decision. If so, supplying him or her with more information than you would need will help you to communicate more effectively.

Often, 'big picture' works for people who are optimistic and enthusiastic—they will run with an idea having understood it at a high level, and they won't worry about how they are going to achieve their desired result, knowing their enthusiasm will see them through. In the meantime, our detail-conscious friends will be looking at all the reasons why it might not work, and thinking that the big-picture idea could be leading them into trouble.

Neither way of thinking is wrong—just different. In an ideal world, both parties would understand their own and each other's preferences and would adjust their communication styles to meet in the middle. We are all capable of every style. Communication is a learnable skill, and when everyone is on the same page, the benefits are incredible.

Can you see how two people might view the same situation from very different perspectives?

'To effectively communicate, we must realise that we are all different in the way we perceive the world and use this understanding as a guide to our communication with others.' – *Tony Robbins, life and business strategist*

Transactional or tailored?

Many organisations are process driven, which can lead clients to feel as though they are part of the process and not valued personally. Processes are important, but when the communication feels robotic and is driven by the organisation's needs rather than the client's, it is incredibly difficult to build relationships. The sustainability of great organisations is based upon building and retaining valued clients. Transactional interactions can leave us feeling cold, whereas tailored approaches will help us feel valued.

Investing in training to develop communication skills within the organisation will result in better service.

CASE STUDY

Going from good to great after scaling up

How do you convince an experienced leadership team that good isn't good enough? From the outside, Band Hatton Button (BHB) looked like a highly successful law firm. Formed from the merger of three legal practices, the company grew and saw good results. They invested in skills and process training, and MD Mark Moseley recognised that to fulfil their purpose of 'delivering excellent legal services with a human touch', they needed to empower staff to focus on relationships rather than just getting business done.

'We have to continue to grow and succeed and develop our team, and to do that we have to invest in the training, the support and the process. When we talk about strategy and where we need to go as an organisation, obviously everything is driven towards where you need to be, and about keeping yourself in business and longevity.

'Some of the very senior guys in terms of experience and age thought they'd been there before, seen it, and done it, so to speak. They were apprehensive and unsure it was necessary for the business. They couldn't necessarily see the benefits. There was enough of the senior team that understood the potential benefits of this or could see its potential. And we had to make sure that we demonstrated the long-term benefit to the business.'

We designed and delivered bespoke training to meet BHB's needs. Every member of their team attended full-day interactive programmes on communication styles. The programmes helped them understand their own styles and their colleagues', and how they could enhance collaboration.

We used DiSC to facilitate this. We also covered how they could better connect with their clients through personalised service based upon each client's communication preference. As well, we helped them identify how to streamline processes to improve client experience and discover tangibles on how to deliver the human touch. We focused on helping them consider the difference between a transactional interaction and a relationship-driven approach.

Mark adds, 'People are more aware now that it's about service. It's about engagement with the clients. It's about flexing, using your style. Another positive that came out of the training is that although we are profiling our staff to be able to work together or work as teams, staff were saying that they can also deduce our clients' preferred communication style and we try to flex our style towards the client. This enables us to give the client the best service that we can possibly give, and make them comfortable and at ease.

'For example, if the lawyers spot that a client values detail and accuracy then they're going to spend time with that client, and give the client the opportunity to consider what they're talking to them about before they rush them into a decision. So their whole process with the client has also changed. This has created lots of discussion around the business and it has created a real energy and buzz around the office.'

Team members have been able to communicate openly and contribute ideas about potential barriers that could be overcome. Here are some of the great changes that have come out of the bespoke programmes: enhanced staff benefits, more team social events, improved internal process and governance and improved facilities for clients.

Staff absence is noticeably reduced, morale is higher and staff are feeling more valued—they are more engaged. As well, client-satisfaction scores are higher.

'Staff is one of our biggest commodities if not the biggest, so in terms of making sure we invest in our people, it's our culture, it is what we believe in and it's what we want to continue to do. And this has obviously been a good investment for the organisation. To be able to bring our people to the level that we want them to be at, but also to give them the confidence and the support they need to do the job we want them to do. So it's been a huge success.'

In your workbook you will find a self-audit. Check how you score on communication skills.
www.firstimpressions.uk.com/trusted

Mastering the art of great communication is a key component of building trust. Getting it wrong can really damage your credibility; getting it right can take you one step closer to finding your T-Spot.

Credibility sleuth

- Show genuine interest in your prospects and clients.

- Spend time and attention on rapport building; this will help you build strong relationships.

- A firm handshake is a must in business. It conveys more about you than you think!

- Respect the time and energy of the person you are communicating with.

- Start to understand people first, rather than expect them to understand you.

- Be flexible with your communication style. The most skilled communicators demonstrate this flexibility.

- Brush up on your body language; it will help you to read others well.

- Consider your speaking style: how you use pitch, rhythm, pace and volume. There is more to your verbal communication than just the words that you use.

- Pay attention to what you are saying without words.

 Credibility thief

- Ignore small talk at your peril.

- Don't overdo the mirroring and matching— it will be too obvious.

- Don't avoid handshakes—you will be seen as less competent and less trustworthy if you do.

- Don't get out of sync with the person you are communicating with.

- Don't steal all the limelight; allow others a chance to shine, too.

- A one-style-fits-all approach to communication will restrict your ability to build strong relationships.

- Don't let your non-verbal communication betray you.

- Avoid filler words and phrases such as 'you know what I mean', 'like', and 'to be honest with you'.

- The message sent isn't always the message received—we all have different filters.

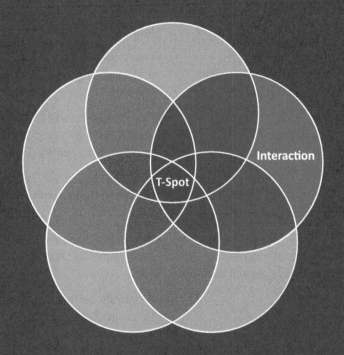

Interaction

T-Spot

Interac

'If people like you, they will listen to you, but if they trust you, they will do business with you.'

– Zig Ziglar, motivational speaker

It takes dedication, energy and thought to create strong, lasting business relationships. We will be successful in business when we consistently focus our attention on the interactions we have. Through interactions, we build and nurture these relationships. Our interactions with colleagues and partners are as important as those with clients and prospects.

Interaction

The importance of building outstanding client relationships

A relationship will not move forward if the other person doesn't like you. You may do some business, but it won't develop into a long-standing relationship. Remember, your clients need to respect you professionally. They need to respect how you carry out your work and also how you treat everyone you interact with.

In February 2017, Uber CEO Travis Kalanick was caught on camera having an argument with his driver. The argument was about Uber's unethical treatment of drivers. Rather than taking the feedback graciously, Kalanick got personal with the driver and the conversation became heated. It was only when the video of the interaction went public that Kalanick issued a statement of apology. It was issued to all staff by email and on the company blog. He said, 'To say that I am ashamed is an extreme understatement. My job as your leader is to lead…and that starts with behaving in a way that makes us all proud.'

Kalanick stepped down as CEO of Uber in June 2017 following pressure from the investors.

Visibility: The paradox of technology

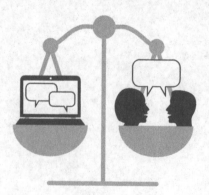

To interact with people, we need to be visible on their radars. Making sure people are aware of you is the first stage of connection; create recognition. The more you are known, the more opportunities will come your way. During the relationship-building phase, it is important to be seen; otherwise, you cannot build credibility.

Visibility is increasingly important as modern working practices become digitised. In one sense, we are more visible than ever before. Yet, we now communicate face-to-face far less often than in previous decades. Technological advances have enabled us to connect with people all over the world, and our virtual presence has increased. This has negatively affected our ability to connect in person and build strong relationships.

'We now have one-twentieth of the interactions with people that we had in 1988!' – *John DiJulius*

Technology enables us to be constantly connected in our personal and professional lives. This can further reduce the number of social interactions we have and make building relationships more difficult. You have most likely seen people sitting with their friends or colleagues in coffee shops glued to their smartphones rather than interacting with each other. We both have teenagers and know first-hand how difficult it is to prise their technology away from them—Heaven forbid they lose their 'streaks' on Snapchat!

There is a blurring of lines. Our work communications can impinge on our social time, and equally, our virtual social networks can erode our working time. We must have clear boundaries regarding how and when we use our technology to benefit our personal and business relationships.
Even MEPs have been caught on social media during parliamentary sessions.

Sarah Windrum, CEO of information technology company Emerald Group, shared this with us: 'Anyone could do IT. It is a commoditised industry. What differentiates us is how we interact and build relationships with our clients. They know that we have their best interests at heart and this results in us building trust.

'We should be the masters of technology; technology should not be the master of us.'

Digitisation: Generational differences

Leaders in today's business environment need to understand how digitisation affects each generation in different ways and, in turn, how we build relationships differently.

BT Research found that 56% of younger managers (aged 18–34) have used video conferencing, compared to 30% of managers over 35. The younger managers feel they can build a similar level of trust in remote relationships, although they also feel that face-to-face is still the best method where possible.

What are the generational differences in approaches to developing relationships in your organisation?

How are you utilising these differences?

How does this affect your client's experience?

We have many options when choosing how to communicate with our clients and colleagues. When making this selection, we must consider cost, time, preference, purpose and the impact we wish to have on the relationship.

Treading a fine line between digitised and personal interactions

Since 2003 Else Solicitors LLP has attributed its growth and success to a single-minded focus on relationship skills—namely networking and collaborating with prospects, introducers and partners.

So how does a firm that prides itself on developing long-standing relationships with clients continue to grow and embrace digitisation without diminishing the value of personal interactions?

In 2012, Oliver Buckle, former head of marketing at Else, began running the monthly professional networking group that attracted members from professional organisations throughout the Midlands. Oliver wanted to create a networking event that wasn't about selling. His vision was to establish a group where relationships mattered. Of course, a networking group would give Else brand exposure, but it had to be about more than just that.

'It was about helping each other, first and foremost. It had to be informal and people had to enjoy themselves.

'We found that simple things matter—being greeted with a smile and a warm welcome; encouraging participants to understand each other's businesses; what motivates them and what their challenges and pains are: events where we all focus on how we can build trust-based relationships, help others first before we try and sell our own services.'

This approach to developing and building relationships runs throughout the firm. A weekly team meeting is held in the boardroom. The purpose of the meeting is to give colleagues a flavour of the types of prospects and businesses the solicitors have spoken with and the stages of these relationships. This identifies potential work and opportunities to create tailored services for clients.

'Referrals and networking are our main source of new business, so there is a strong focus on training and development for all team members. Some of the team find it easier than others. Developing our relationship-building skills, being prepared and having an idea of key topics to discuss all help with confidence prior to face-to-face meetings.'

Else has embraced digitisation by implementing a customer relationship management (CRM) system, marketing automation that supports face-to-face interactions. This has come with its own challenges, particularly in an established team whose vision and values centre on their ability to develop long-standing relationships. Oliver has focused on ensuring that the system adds value to the client experience and doesn't detract from it.

'Having an understanding of how to best use the information we have from prospects and how to nurture the relationship further allows us to bring more value to the client and ongoing revenue to our firm. We might decide to send our prospects a useful guide, put them in touch with a technical specialist or invite them to one of our networking or hospitality events.'

At Else, it's not about replacing personal interactions with digitisation. It's about getting the balance right and embracing both. It's about understanding when to communicate electronically and when to communicate and develop the relationship at a much more personal level. A clear strategy on how to build and manage relationships at all stages and levels is something that the team takes seriously; it is not left to chance.

'Used correctly, and [when we pay] particular attention to the analytics, marketing automation is beneficial for our valued clients and profitable for our business. Being consistent with our brand message through our people and being clear on how we build relationships across the business will continue to be a priority as our business grows.'

The power of face-to-face

According to a study conducted at Beijing Normal University, face-to-face communication differs from other forms of communication in two ways:

◊ it involves integrating 'multimodal sensory information' (facial gestures), and
◊ it involves more turn-taking between participants, which has been shown to play a pivotal role in interactions.

Further research by Alex (Sandy) Pentland—professor and director of MIT Human Dynamics Lab—published in the *International Journal of Organisational Design*, shows that meeting in person allows for more eye contact, which builds trust and encourages group members to confide in and co-create with their group.

'The more team members directly interact with each other face-to-face, and the more they trust other team members, the more creative and of higher quality their teamwork is.' – *Sandy Pentland*

Leaders from some of the most successful organisations in the world have encouraged their teams to interact face-to-face more often. The late Steve Jobs of Apple was passionate about colleague interaction. He designed workspaces to facilitate in-person interactions.

Our client Audit Scotland provides audit services for the public sector. Many of their auditors work remotely and are based all over Scotland. One of their initiatives to increase employee interaction is a Lunch and Learn session, which everyone can attend. It involves watching TED Talks and then asking employees to offer perspectives on the concepts.

Another initiative is Learning and Innovation Groups. The participants run with a topic and feed the ideas to the leadership group. For example, the participants may discuss the future of auditing following the publication of an industry report.

The groups are self-formed, self-facilitated and both horizontally and vertically diverse, encouraging interaction across the organisation. As the groups develop internal relationship skills informally, they also develop employees' ability to grow client relationships, too.

We realise that face-to-face communication is not always possible, but there are times when it is essential. A senior leader in professional services recently told us that when it matters, he knows he has to arrange to fly out to see his clients, even if that means a round trip of ten hours for a one-hour meeting: 'There are times when it is important to look them in the eye.'

The human moment

Being physically present and giving emotional and intellectual attention is what psychiatrist Edward Hallowell calls 'the human moment'.

'It's an authentic psychological encounter that can happen only when two people share the same physical space. I have given it a name because I believe that it has started to disappear from modern life—and I sense that we may all be about to discover the destructive power of its absence.'

Human moments don't have to be long to be effective. You could sit next to someone on a transatlantic flight and share the physical space but not the emotional space. To make the human moment work, you need to be totally present with the person you are communicating with, avoiding all distractions so that your energy is felt and a connection is made. This could be as simple as a quick chat while making a drink in the kitchen at work, or a more formal session.

Since these moments cannot happen through remote working, it is all the more important to take time to re-connect with both your colleagues and clients. Remember, the more visible you are, the better the connections you're going to make with your clients. World-class organisations break down barriers by moving from transactional interactions to meaningful client relationships.

A lack of human moments can create barriers between organisations and their clients. When banks introduced ATMs and clients no longer required personal service, the whole lending process became more difficult for both the bank and the client. Familiarity and therefore trust were absent. Banks are now trying to find new ways of getting to know their customers and building relationships.

'For business to do well, you can't have high tech without high touch. They have to work together.' – *Edward Hallowell, psychiatrist*

Environment

It is important to understand how our environment can influence the strength of our interactions. If we are not comfortable in our surroundings, this can negatively affect our behaviour and the other person's. Things to consider:

◊ location and time
◊ client's preference
◊ suitability of the meeting place for the intended discussion
◊ formality of the environment, and
◊ layout of the room.

What does being visible mean to you?

In a changing environment, how do you ensure your visibility?

What steps are you going to take to ensure you are continually connected to your clients?

Credibility

While building visibility, we also need to build credibility. Credibility is built up over time as clients and colleagues get to know you. In her book *Presence*, Amy Cuddy shows that trust is characterised by warmth. Respect is characterised by competence and knowledge. At the beginning of a relationship, it is important to establish that trust and respect. The ability to position yourself with graceful authority is a learnable skill.

You may need to position yourself differently depending on context and environment (while remaining authentic). For example, if you were leading a meeting, you would need to position yourself in a way that demonstrated your skills and ability in that context. But if you were with a client from a particular industry, you would need to focus on your relevant experience in that sector, demonstrating empathy for the client.

This positioning skill is essential during interactions.

> It's about being chameleon-like with honesty and integrity—never lying, but knowing which aspects of your background to play up or down to best fit the situation.

As human beings we are complex characters with diamond-like facets. If we showed all of our facets at once it would be overwhelming!

This is about more than building rapport—it's about quickly identifying the characteristics and gestures that will help the relationship progress. You are looking for signals, patterns and a connection with your client or audience. Observing body language, verbal language and voice quality will help you determine whether you are hitting the mark or whether you need to move on.

CASE STUDY

Building trust through quality interactions

Birmingham Optical Group Ltd, established in 1967, is a principal supplier of high-quality instruments and machines to the ophthalmic profession. When CEO Steve Fleming joined the business in 2016, he soon realised that customers were buying based on the strength of the products and not on the strength of after-sales service or relationships.

Following extensive customer satisfaction and staff-engagement surveys, it was evident that unless significant changes were made, the business would flounder.

'It was clear from our customer satisfaction surveys that the propensity to repurchase was low and that if I didn't sit up and take note then the business would die. I realised that I needed to address whether our people had the right capabilities to move the business forward. Employees with an excess of 30 years' service had only a year's worth of experience as they hadn't been developed or empowered and they weren't clear on how they could contribute to the customer experience.'

Steve identified that relationships needed to be strengthened both internally and externally. He introduced initiatives to build trust internally that improved his team's motivation and performance, as well as the quality of their interactions.

'When I joined the company, the office-based staff had to clock in daily and field-based staff had trackers fitted on their vehicles. These practices were immediately removed. If we can't trust our staff then how can we expect them to build trusted relationships with our customers? The strength of these relationships and delivering excellent service are the biggest marketing opportunities we have.'

In the preceding five years there had been five different service managers in the business. Steve personally recruited a new service manager who had operational and behavioural skills that aligned with his vision.

'Historically, the company had panic-recruited to fill vacancies. Our strength moving forward will be ensuring our people have the human skills they need to develop excellent business relationships. We have to be consistent in our approach as our customers expect a high level of expertise and service from us. Our interactions should not be focused on selling products but on becoming trusted advisers. It is our responsibility to use our professional judgement to guide and inform our customers in order that they can make good buying decisions and plan their future expenditure.'

By shadowing some of his employees, Steve has been able to witness first-hand some of the difficulties and frustrations that create barriers to building outstanding relationships. Empowering his team to share stories with each other and with the executive team has significantly affected how his team members treat each other and how they interact and build relationships with their customers.

'The tone and spirit within our company has been improved. When we have happy staff we have happy customers. We are now building better relationships because we are seeing issues from the customer's perspective. It's not enough to know our customers— they have to like us to want to continue to do business with us.'

Steve shared an example of how he plans and prepares for his business interactions. On a recent business trip to Tokyo, he was aware that the trip's success would be dependent on how well he could connect and build trust in a relatively short period of time. Being fully prepared was crucial. Understanding the differences in culture and how the team would handle the interactions was an important part of the planning process.

'I didn't leave anything to chance and knew how important this business trip was. I knew who was going to be in the room, what types of personalities they had, their history and background. I respected their knowledge as, in Japan, many employees have been with the same company for most of their working lives.

'During the interactions I was aware of their expectations of me and which characteristics they were expecting to see, to show tha I was credible. At times I had to demonstrate my assertiveness and confidence and at others being humble was more appropriat When I delivered a presentation, it wasn't enough to show that I was knowledgeable—being able to listen and handle objections a remain calm were also important. Having this awareness and bein able to modify your behaviour to build the relationship requires a l of planning and self-reflection.'

Birmingham Optical has seen improved ratings for customer satisfaction and staff engagement during the past 12 months and is now in a much stronger position. A focus on people developme and building trust internally will ensure that internal and external relationships are further strengthened.

Credibility statement

Whenever you meet someone for the first time, the inevitable question comes up: 'What do you do?' Whethe you are networking, at an interview, meeting in social circles, attending a conference or just waiting in line at the supermarket checkout, this question tends to crop up.

People in business development roles understand the pow of positioning themselves with a creditability statement. Bu many people shy away from this, feeling it is 'too salesy'. Therefore, their response to the question may be awkward; they may feel unprepared and waffle on with no structure.

Effectively, we are all sales people. Whether you are in a support role or front line, many business opportunities will come from the people you know. Therefore, all individuals in an organisation should be prepared to step up and deliver a professional credibility statement that reflects the knowledge, qualities and personality, and that positions their organisation favourably.

When credibility statements are delivered well, doors to more meaningful interactions are opened. Through our work, we have observed that people are often reticent about carrying out a credibility-statement exercise. But once they have completed the process, we can see that it

◊ increases confidence
◊ creates a more positive energy
◊ positions everyone in the organisation as valuable
◊ highlights pride in the organisation, and
◊ encourages teamwork.

During a visit to the NASA space centre in 1962, President John F. Kennedy noticed a caretaker sweeping the floor. He said to the man, 'Hi, I'm Jack Kennedy. What are you doing?'

'Well, Mr President, I'm helping put a man on the moon,' the caretaker responded.

In many people's eyes, the NASA caretaker was just cleaning the building. But he understood that he was helping to make history. He understood the vision and his part in it, and he had a purpose.

A similar story is of Christopher Wren, one of the greatest English architects. One day he was walking, unrecognised, by the men building St Paul's cathedral in London, which he designed.

'What are you doing?' he asked one of the workmen. The man replied, 'I'm cutting a piece of stone.' As he walked, Christopher asked another man the same question, and the man replied, 'I'm earning five shillings two pence a day.'

He asked a third man the same question, and the man answered, 'I am helping Sir Christopher Wren build a beautiful cathedral.'

That man had the vision. He could see beyond the cutting of stone, beyond the earning of his daily wage, to the creation of a work of art—the building of a great cathedral.

'Whatever role you hold within an organisation, your contribution is essential to its success. When a whole team demonstrates this type of attitude and commitment to the purpose of the organisation, amazing things happen.'
– © First Impressions Training

> '**Credibility consists of three aspects: good sense, good will, good moral character.**'
> – *Aristotle*

Tips on writing your credibility statement

If you are a leader, manager or business owner and want to accelerate your business growth, know that a credibility statement is fundamental to your success. Everyone should have one, and should practice the delivery until it comes naturally. This credibility-statement exercise will ensure that employees know how to introduce themselves in any setting and will help them feel more comfortable talking about their work. Don't underestimate the power of a well-delivered credibility statement. Even those team members who are not in front-line positions can still affect your brand.

What to include

A credibility statement should typically last up to 60 seconds. It may be slightly shorter, or longer, depending on the context. If you are in a job interview or presenting to an audience, you might include additional content. Generally shorter is better to hold the other person's interest.

The following are a few ways to develop your credibility statement.

◊ Start by thinking about why you do what you do. What is it that gets you out of bed in the morning, and what do you love about your job? Simon Sinek, in his famous TedX Talk and his book *Start With Why*, says, 'People don't buy what you do, they buy why you do it. And what you do simply proves what you believe.'

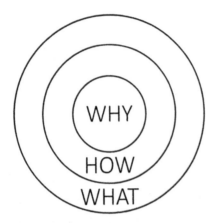

◊ Establish your authority by demonstrating previous experience or knowledge: 'For 10 years I have been inspired to...'
◊ Consider what others can learn from you and not from anyone else.
◊ Think about the difference you can make for your clients—the pain points you can resolve.
◊ Use powerful language; for example, words such as 'inspire', 'passionate', 'desire', 'belief', 'understand'.
◊ Make sure it is quite conversational—not a hard sell.
◊ Talk about shared beliefs or values.
◊ Link to the purpose of the organisation you work for.
◊ Think about your energy, your body language and your gestures. It will not come across well if you say 'I'm passionate about...' in a monotone voice with no passion!

 In your workbook you will find space to answer questions that will help you to formulate your own credibility statement.
www.firstimpressions.uk.com/trusted/

How well do your team members deliver their credibility statements?

Client intelligence

In a world-class organisation, service is tailored to the client— it is not one-size-fits-all.

'Clients who are made to feel important will be easier to work with.' – *Tony Cram, programme director, Ashridge Business School*

We are not talking about gaining insights to be able to sell more. We are talking about building rapport, interacting, building relationships, engaging on a human level and making a connection. Gathering and utilising client intelligence data can help you better understand your client's activities, preferences, likes and dislikes in a personal context. You can then use this information to personalise your service to best meet their needs. This must be done with sincerity and integrity, with the intention of helping the client to feel important, not just as a logical data-collection exercise.

How to gather client intelligence

Pick up on the cues that people volunteer by using your peripheral vision and heightened senses. People will give you insight into what is important to them; you just need to watch for it. This type of information becomes more valuable as the relationship progresses.

> 'The key to building great relationships is making the other person happy to see you. If they are not, you are always swimming against the tide. When I go to see long-standing clients, even before we speak about business, they want a few minutes to catch up, have a drink and talk about their personal interests. I am happy to see them and they are happy to see me. You get a level of trust that you can't get through pure facts and figures or pricing. Without that level of trust, you cannot retain clients year after year.' – Pete Hall, managing director, 2 Blues Ltd.

For example, say your client has children, and in a conversation, he mentions that he collects them from nursery at the end of the day. If you constantly suggest a wash-up meeting with him at the end of the day, this will not build a good relationship. It would be much better to suggest an alternative time of day.

Knowing whether your client prefers to communicate face-to-face or by telephone, email, text or conference call is very helpful as well. If you constantly contact her in her preferred way, you will automatically build a better relationship with her.

Understanding how your client wishes to develop the relationship—outside of buying a product or service—will enhance the connection and fast-track the relationship. In our experience, this understanding is often overlooked.

Hot-desking or working from home are becoming more popular in organisations. It is therefore even more important to consult with the client on how he or she wishes to communicate. A change in working practices must not be detrimental to the client.

During these conversations, the client will also pick up your cues and find out more about you. They have to admire the whole you, not just the work you. They will learn about your hobbies and interests, whether you volunteer outside of work and about the quality of your personal relationships, too. All of this information will help them build their relationship with you. Building a relationship is a two-way interaction. If it is purely one-sided, the relationship will not grow.

Over time, many business relationships develop into friendships. In some sectors you may even attend corporate hospitality events and meet clients' families. This will deepen the relationship as well. Of course, in some instances or sectors where clients' professional independence is a key value, this may not happen to the same degree.

Relationships must be enhanced, not reduced.

One of our professional services clients recently shared a story with us about her client meetings. She sees great value in communicating with her clients in a way that best suits them. She tailors her approach to meet their preferences— this is of paramount importance to her. Colleagues questioned why she needed to have a fortnightly meeting with one of her clients, and she told us that she gained more value from the two-hour meeting every fortnight than any number of emails and phone calls could have provided. The face-to-face interaction has developed an open and transparent relationship in which she truly became a trusted advisor.

It is also important to remember that small acts of kindness can make all the difference to the connections you make and the interactions you have. The intention of a kind act should not be to get something in return; it should be purely to enhance the connection you have with your prospect, client or colleague. If it is not done with sincerity, the recipient will not feel the warmth of your communication. When there is incongruence, trust can easily be broken.

Donna's story   The staff at the local coffee shop always know which drinks my son and I are going to order. They also know my son is a wheelchair user, and that he likes to order the drinks but can't physically carry them. They always offer to carry the drinks over to the table. This allows Harvey to feel that he has been able to buy the drinks and take them to his mum. What they do is simple, but it does make us feel special. We know that they have remembered us and our needs and that they are interested enough to care. It makes us feel valued as customers.

We all feel the benefit of a kind act, whether we are the giver or the receiver.

Recording client intelligence

The information could be recorded in a formal company-wide system, such as a CRM system, or simply as individual notes in a consultant's notebook. If the information is in a CRM system, the wider team can access it. In an organisation where several team members may be working for the same client, this can be a great way of sharing the information.

We've seen recording systems ranging from one extreme to another. Some people keep the information in their heads, some make notes in their email systems next to the contact's name, and some have fields in their CRM to capture the information. It is of course essential to comply with data protection laws.

'There is no financial cost to gathering client intelligence, but the impact it can make on the client relationship and how it makes the client feel is a priceless intangible asset.'
– © *First Impressions Training*

FIRST formula

We have developed our FIRST Formula to remind you of what might be important to your client.

F – Family

I – Interests

R – Recreation

S – Specific preferences

T – Topical

This information should NOT be gathered in a checklist style! It will be gifted to you over time during conversations with your client—through small talk. Remembering that your client's son Freddie has just started university and asking how he is getting on will make all the difference to the interaction you have.

How could this information be recorded and shared in your organisation?

What do you currently capture and record?

How could you build a client intelligence system with the sole intention of having better interactions?

> **'Respect is earned, honesty is appreciated, trust is gained, loyalty is returned.'**
> *– Unknown*

Networking

We know that building connections, interacting, and developing relationships are integral to growing a business. For some of us, networking skills are intuitive, but for others, they don't come naturally at all. The ability to network effectively is a learnable skill, and one that can reap great rewards with targeted effort.

BT Research predicts that it will become an even more important skill as a greater number of younger business managers turn to networking to secure new business partnerships. Fifty-seven percent of business managers aged 18 to 34 meet potential clients through networking events, compared to 29% of managers over 35. Networking events are especially popular with larger companies—over 50% of businesses with more than 50 employees use networking events to meet potential clients or suppliers.

We want to share some of our top tips from our own experience, highlighting where the credibility thief may strike!

Networking tips

Planning

Spend a little time planning before the event to ensure you maximise your valuable time when networking.

◊ Ensure your LinkedIn profile is up to date and that it accurately represents you and your brand.

◊ Obtain the guest list, decide who you wish to connect with and check out their profiles on LinkedIn. See *Element 4: Behaviour—Behaviour in communication*.

◊ Research the format of the event, identify dress-code requirements and plan what you will wear. See *Element 5: Professional image—Dress codes*.

◊ Make sure your credibility statement is prepared. See *Credibility statement*, earlier in this section.

◊ Remember your business cards.

◊ Be clear on the types of connections you wish to make—it will be difficult for people to introduce you if you're vague.

◊ Manage your nerves—if you find networking daunting, you will find plenty of tips in *Element 1: Mindset—Overcoming mindset barriers*.

◊ Mention on social media that you are looking forward to attending the event—it will help people to connect with you.

During the event

We could write a whole book on the behaviour we see while networking! To protect the innocent (or not so innocent), we have written in general terms about the things we have witnessed.

Things to remember

• Assess the situation. Be aware of what is going on in the room. Look at the groups. It is much easier to join a group of three rather than a pair who might be engaged in a personal conversation.

• Create a great first impression. For more details, see *Element 2* and *Element 5*. Remember the basics: walk in confidently, smile, make eye contact and give a firm handshake.

- Refer to people by name. If you have a poor memory, there is no harm in asking someone to repeat his or her name.
- Make small talk before business talk, and then balance social and business conversation.
- Listen attentively and avoid jumping in with advice before you are aware of all of the facts.
- Be focused, engaged and attentive—the recipient will know if you are not and this will break trust.
- Use a range of questioning techniques when interacting to find out more and build a greater connection. Include precision questions such as 'Whom would it be useful for me to connect with?' (A precision question helps you get to the point quickly and therefore improves communication efficiency and critical thinking.)
- Be a connector; help people by connecting those who would be useful contacts for each other.
- Speak about others as you would if they were in the room.
- Be kind and gracious. Think about how you can help others first.

Things to avoid

- Don't be a business-card thruster! You know the type— the moment you walk through the door they offer you a business card without even attempting to interact.
- Don't deliver a poor introduction. This is your opportunity to shine; use it wisely.
- Avoid turning your back on people.
- Don't leave people out. If you spot someone trying to join your conversation, allow her in. Don't leave her standing there feeling awkward.
- Avoid poor handshakes. We covered handshake avoidance and the art of good handshakes thoroughly in *Element 2*.
- Avoid sabotaging your personal brand and your organisational brand through inappropriate behaviour.
- Don't gossip.

- Don't talk only about yourself—ask questions to build engagement.
- Avoid coming across as desperate. Trying to sell instead of trying to connect is inappropriate.
- Don't be disrespectful or rude to other attendees in a similar line of business.
- Don't treat people as if they are insignificant; everyone is there to promote their businesses.

Follow-up

You have spent time planning, and you have spent time at the networking event. Now, it's just as important to spend time following up with your new connections. Otherwise, attending the event could have been a waste of your time.

◊ Join your new contacts on LinkedIn or other social media and professional networking sites and send a follow-up message. Do not attempt to sell in this message. This will break trust and switch the person off. We have been on the receiving end of selling emails many times and they rarely work—and they can damage your credibility.

◊ Do what you said you would do. If you promised to send some information, connect someone or arrange a coffee, do it! The failure to follow up on your promises will break trust immediately and may jeopardise any further connection.

◊ Record client intelligence data for future use.

'When you make a commitment you create hope. When you keep a commitment you create trust.' – *John C. Maxwell, leadership speaker*

CASE STUDY

Getting on the radar

Award-winning networker and marketing professional Henrik Court believes that networking is about getting on others' radar, staying on it by making yourself memorable and easy to do business with. Building relationships, establishing needs and providing solutions all stem from interacting with people.

Henrik says, 'I refer to it as sowing seeds. The more people I interact with, the more I can help others, and in turn I can be helped.'

During an interview he attended many years ago, Henrik was asked about his ability to network.

'At this stage of my career, I hadn't attended any networking events as they were not common business practice. I was honest in my response but added that if I went into a room with six friends and there were six hundred people in the room, at the end of the evening, I would be the one who would have talked to the most people.'

He got the job!

According to Henrik, fundamentally, business is about people. People make up organisations, and if we spend time really getting to know the people, seeing how they operate, we can anticipate their behaviour and it becomes easier to do business with them. Henrik says, 'Business is also about providing solutions. The more you get to know and understand your network's issues, the easier it is to identify how you can help people.'

He believes that it's important to choose the right type of networking event in order to catch up with existing contacts, build your contact list or broaden your knowledge.

'It's not about the number of people in the room. Whether it is a formal event with a speaker and dinner or an informal breakfast meeting, a networking event should be an experience where people can share ideas, interact and build relationships. There is no set formula—it's about finding the types of events that work for you.' He adds, 'When I organise events, I want people to see a return on their investment. Providing quality venues, speakers and appetising food sets the tone for a relaxed atmosphere in which business relationships can be fostered. Part of my role is to help connect people in the room and to encourage them to connect others in return.'

Henrik explains that building up a database of contacts isn't about adding numbers. Thousands of connections are merely connections if a relationship is not developed. Keeping in regular contact through telephone conversations, catching up at events or arranging meetups will ensure the relationship is maintained. He believes that it doesn't matter where these people are located in the world—what matters is that you build on the initial connection.

'Many of these people may never be your clients, but they may lead you to clients through their connections. Like anything in life that's worth having, relationships take time and effort to develop and need to be nurtured in order to be fruitful. They should be mutually beneficial.'

How could you improve networking skills in your organisation?

 In your workbook you will find a checklist to help you achieve networking success, as well as a self-audit. Check how you score on interaction skills.
www.firstimpressions.uk.com/trusted/

Mastering the art of great interaction is a key component of building trust. Getting it wrong can really damage your credibility; getting it right can take you one step closer to finding your T-Spot.

Credibility sleuth

- Find the right balance between technology and face-to-face interactions.

- Encourage 'water-cooler' moments in organisations. Innovation can happen through these interactions.

- Know which characteristics and gestures will be helpful for each interaction.

- Position yourself with gracious authority in your credibility statement to connect with your audience.

- Tailor your approach to best work with the recipient.

- Pick up on information gifted by your contacts and consider how to utilise client intelligence to further your relationships.

- Take a planned approach to networking.

- Be kind and gracious—how can you help others first when networking?

- Do what you said you would do.

- Consider your surroundings and how you can nurture a relationship in the environment.

Credibility thief

- Technology alone will not result in strong, trusted relationships.

- Both innovation and productivity are stifled without enough 'human moments'.

- If you are fake or false, this will show through and damage your credibility.

- When you inadequately position yourself, you miss opportunities.

- A one-size-fits-all approach does not work in world-class relationships.

- Don't interrogate your clients! This needs to be a subtle activity.

- Without a systematic approach, you could end up spending lots of time drinking coffee but not strengthening your relationships!

- Avoid trying to sell instead of trying to connect—you will come across as desperate.

- Don't over promise and under deliver.

- If a client is uncomfortable or the surroundings are not conducive to the activity you are undertaking, the relationship will flounder.

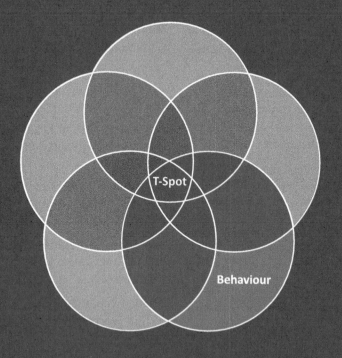

T-Spot

Behaviour

'I've learned that people will forget what you said, people will forget what you did, but people will never forget how you made them feel.'

– Maya Angelou, civil rights activist

In business, we must differentiate ourselves through our brand, through our product offering and, in a service business in particular, through the behaviour of our people. Your clients' perceptions of your organisation are developed through the people they interact with in your company.

Behaviour

Managing behaviour

Managing behaviour and aligning it with your organisation's values positively impacts on the client experience. In turn, this will drive company growth and give you a competitive advantage.

Leaders within the organisation need to model the desired behaviours. Telling people what is required doesn't work; employees' behaviour must be reinforced through leaders' actions.

The *Journal of Applied Psychology* published a study with strong evidence supporting the idea that leading by example gets others to engage in desired behaviours; group members were more likely to engage in a desired behaviour if they saw a leader they identified with doing the same.

'Setting an example is not the main means of influencing others; it is the only means.'
– Albert Einstein

CASE STUDY
Managing behaviour in the moment

Nigel Bromley, client services director of brand consultancy Key Parker, says, 'I was told, many years ago by a colleague, that at the heart of managing a professional relationship is the fact that it happens in the moment.

'That's why it can be so rewarding and so stressful. You have to make decisions on how to behave, how to react and how to navigate personalities, remembering that you are representing the company and may have to provide a professional opinion that your client may find challenging.

'It is vital that you master the interpersonal skills to be able to manage yourself and understand and effectively communicate with your clients.

'But, more critically, you must work in an environment that is open and supportive of your role. At Key Parker, we all prepare thoroughly for meetings. We work as a group to review client emails, instructions and concerns. We also work together to develop the response. This collaborative approach teaches everyone how to prepare and how to behave in a way that is both caring for the client and professional in behaviour.'

The proof that this works for Key Parker is that their client relationships are measured in decades rather than years, all of their business is derived from referrals and staff turnover is less than 5%. These metrics reveal a successful consultancy-based business.

Managing negative behaviour

Negative behaviour should not only be addressed during disciplinary or appraisal processes—it should be consistently reviewed, and any required changes should be acted upon immediately.

> American entertainment company Netflix has nine core values—behaviours and skills that are valued in employees. One of these is 'courage', and a key expectation connected to this value is that employees 'question actions inconsistent with [the company's] values and behaviours'.

All employees should be empowered to highlight negative behaviour that impacts on client relationships or the organisation's internal culture.

Setting behaviour expectations

In every business, team members should know how they are expected to behave, and should be aware of the impact their behaviour has on client and colleague interactions.

'How well a company is doing now is measured by sales; how well a company will do in the future is measured by client satisfaction.' — © First Impressions Training

Anderson, Fornell and Lehmann carried out research into the economic benefits of improving customer satisfaction. They determined that for every 1% per year increase in customer satisfaction over a five-year period, there is a cumulative increase of 11.5% in net profitability. The findings support the idea that improved service increases customer satisfaction and, in turn, profitability.

Creating an internal culture with a client-centric service vision

There are great benefits to building an internal culture that recognises high standards of behaviour.

Many organisations place trust, integrity and respect high on their list of values, and state that it is important to reflect these values internally as well as with clients. It is not enough to just quote these values on websites or in reception areas; the values must be truly lived and breathed.

Enron, an American energy, commodities and services company, went bankrupt as a result of fraudulent activity. The company's values were displayed in client-facing areas, and these included 'integrity' and 'respect'. These values were clearly not part of the culture at Enron; they were merely words on the wall.

Implementing positive behaviour to support organisational values will result in:

- increased employee engagement
- fewer absences
- improved teamwork
- happy and fulfilled employees
- increased productivity and performance
- mutual respect

- an enhanced reputation
- higher client retention rates
- loyalty
- cross-selling opportunities for future revenue
- increased market share, and
- lower employee turnover due to happy teams.

'There cannot be two opposing cultures in an organisation. How we treat our employees will be how they, in turn, treat our clients.' — © *First Impressions Training*

A service vision with the client right at the centre will emphasise to your team the importance of behavioural skills, and will elevate their service-aptitude skills. To achieve long-term sustainability in business, you have to focus on developing a strong internal culture and behavioural skills that will differentiate your business.

Positive behaviours

Here are some ways to implement positive behaviours in your organisation.

- Reinforce positive behaviour by acknowledging and appreciating good work.
- Involve people in discussions that affect them—empowerment leads to a happier workforce.

- Create a culture of giving and receiving feedback.
- Ensure leaders model good behaviour and don't just demand it.
- Respond to others' ideas positively; don't shoot them down.
- Encourage healthy conflict and debate.
- Commit to moving forward collectively when an agreement has been reached.
- Take responsibility and be accountable.
- Create a no-blame culture—update training, processes and procedures as necessary to ensure lessons learned are incorporated into the culture.
- Make sure clients can align themselves with the company's morals and ethics.
- Encourage punctuality and attendance—these drive a great culture.
- Pay attention to detail.
- Remove any barriers in the business (see *Removing barriers*, later in this section) and make it easy for your clients to do business with you.

Non-negotiable standards

Non-negotiable standards of behaviour are those standards that everyone in a company is expected to operate at. Everyone should be aware of these standards, and the example should be set from the top down. Many standards will vary from business to business, albeit some will be universal. Here are some examples of non-negotiable standards.

◊ Always speaking to colleagues when passing them in the corridors or communal areas—getting to know colleagues across the business will encourage teamwork and collaboration.

◊ Eating lunch away from your desk and in a communal area—not only does taking a physical break from the workspace encourage relationship building, it also increases productivity. People will return to their workspace refreshed and ready to work.

◊ Being honest and transparent with clients (this should be a non-negotiable standard in all organisations)—even when something goes wrong, agree to have an open and honest conversation. This will demonstrate integrity, enhance the relationship and your reputation. Your patterns of behaviour will defy you if you are being dishonest.

◊ Having a team huddle first thing in the morning to establish goals and highlight issues—this will help motivate the team and ensure that each team member knows the part he or she is playing each day, resulting in improved performance.

We find that companies often think they have non-negotiable standards in place, but when we work with them, many issues are raised that demonstrate this isn't the case!

 What non-negotiable standards could be implemented in your organisation?

'When organisations are clear on their non-negotiable standards, this helps them to build and protect a compelling culture.'
— © First Impressions Training

CASE STUDY

Keeping a family culture while expanding the business

The Eden Hotel Collection started out as one hotel—Mallory Court, in Warwick. The collection has now grown to a portfolio of nine beautiful and carefully chosen hotels. Each one has been selected for the unique qualities it offers: beautiful architecture, outstanding food, peaceful surroundings and the sense of total escape and relaxation offered to each and every guest who steps into the hotel.

While each property in the collection has its own character and personality, all uphold the impeccable standards of service, quality and attention to detail for which the Eden Hotel Collection is renowned.

Eden is part of the larger Rigby Group, but they strive to maintain a small-company culture. So how does Eden keep a family feel, which is one of their core values, as they grow and develop as a business?

Sales and marketing director Tara Robinson says, 'We keep a family feel by building familiarity—the really simple things, such as communicating who has started at each hotel, so as employees we all know each other. Some hotels hold a family day each year to celebrate together, involving partners and children. It allows us to show our appreciation to everyone.

'Our general manager at Mallory Court has been with us for 26 years, and our head housekeeper has been with us for just under 30 years. It's really important to share these stories to our new team members to show that there is longevity to the business. Many of the head office team have also been here 10 to 15 years too, so we have all grown with the development of the business. It gives people a real feel for their future development when they join the Eden family. We are firm believers in promoting from within and have many success stories.'

Tara started her career as cabin crew for Virgin. 'All airlines do customer-service training really well as you are in a metal tube at 37,000 feet, so there is no room for error.' Much of what Tara learned in her first customer-service role stands her in good stead today. When it comes to dealing with customer-service issues, she advises the following:

- discuss the issue in a private area away from an audience
- empathise
- listen, really well
- apologise
- follow up, and
- do something extra—especially if something has gone wrong.

'Many people who work in a customer-service industry really enjoy pleasing people and doing a great job. That's certainly what still makes me tick. The best reward is when someone writes a note or sends a card or an email to thank me or the team for our service.'

Eden runs an internal training system, Red Star, to provide a foundation for exceptional service standards. Tara tells us, 'One of the key aspects of that is anticipation, almost reading the guest's mind. I consider that as more than going the extra mile. It's remembering their preferences if they have visited previously. We have a really high number of return guests, so we aim to personalise the service. All of our team members stay at our hotels as guests and dine as guests—and give feedback—so they can see and feel exactly what the experience is like. It then motivates them to deliver excellent service because they understand how it feels to receive the experience themselves.

'We like to "surprise and delight" our guests too. In a world of fairly routine predictability, we like to add an element of surprise. We might bring in ice-cream to a corporate training session if it is a hot day, or put flowers or chocolates in a guest's room, for example.

'It's important to feel valued, rather than just one of a number. Our team is then able to deliver that care and attention that comes from a personal ownership and a group of highly capable, dedicated professionals who care about their product and service and the performance of the business.'

Doing the right thing

Doing the right thing should not be simply part of a process; it should be a habit for all team members, woven into everything they do. It's being able to stand in your client's shoes and make a decision in that moment. It's about surprising your client in a positive way. Doing the right thing is often not expensive for the organisation, but it is priceless for clients. They will tell everyone they meet about their experience.

It is the people within organisations who interact with clients, not the company itself, so it makes sense to recruit people with an aptitude for good service. Those with an inherent ability to connect well with clients and provide legendary service would score high in service-aptitude tests. It is the company's responsibility to ensure staff are trained in client service—it shouldn't be left to chance.

'Service aptitude is a person's ability to recognise opportunities to exceed customers' expectations, regardless of the circumstances.' – *John DiJulius*

In your workbook you will find a service-aptitude test to complete for your organisation.
www.firstimpressions.uk.com/trusted/

CASE STUDY
PRIDE in their legendary service

As part of their PRIDE statement, Nationwide Building Society challenges their employees to demonstrate their values through actions. We love this story, which was shared with us by Lucy Barton, senior membership value propositions manager, and Lauren Ward, management trainee. Lauren helped a member in need, and this story really shows how they 'do the right thing' and provide legendary service for their members.

'A member came into the branch looking to get an overdraft. I checked her profile and found she was not eligible for one. When I told her this, she looked quite panicked, so I had a look at her eligibility for a personal loan or a credit card. When I found out that she would not be eligible for these products either, I took her into a private room to tell her the news.

'Upon hearing the news, she burst into tears. I got her some tissues and asked her why she was looking for an overdraft. She said that she needed the money for the first three weeks of her university course (to pay rent and buy groceries, etc.), as her student loan wasn't due to be paid into her account until three weeks after her course start date.

'When it became clear that she did not have any family or friends who were in a position to support her financially, I had a look online at the UCAS and Student Finance websites to see if there was any information on financial aid. I found a phone number to call and spoke to Student Finance on her behalf (as she was very shy and didn't want to talk to anyone over the phone).

'Student Finance advised me to print out a form to apply for emergency funding, and they also suggested I contact the member's university. I printed off the form and offered to call her university, but she wanted to apply via Student Finance first before looking elsewhere. She thanked me as she left the branch and I asked her to come into the branch again if she needed any further help.'

This simple gesture of kindness and goodwill is immeasurable in terms of the value it has added to Nationwide Building Society's reputation. It certainly will have strengthened the relationship with this member, and will have increased the likelihood that she will be a loyal, long-standing member. It will also have boosted the happiness hormone, oxytocin, in the member of staff who carried out the gesture of kindness. This will further reinforce her loyalty as an employee, so it is a win-win!

Substantiated value

Very often organisations think their employees are offering world-class service to their clients, when in fact they are merely delivering what is expected. It's only when a client feels he has received something over and above the standard expected that he will be enthused about your business and recommend your services. This level of trust is evoked through your behaviours and actions. Your clients are looking for substantiated value in exchange for the money they spend.

> Andrew Haworth, managing director of Bartle Hall Hotel, Lancashire, told us, 'If the guest positively thanks us and recommends us, then we have done a great job. Unless that recognition is there, we haven't done enough.'

What initiatives have you taken to deliver legendary service? What are you doing to ensure this happens more often?

Client expectations of a global organisation

How does a global technology company continually meet and exceed its clients' high expectations?

The bar is set very high and there is a long way to fall if expectations are not met. During our recent interview with Dominic Myles, a former European services leader at IBM, he told us, 'I have never worked in any other company where expectations are set high before we even walk through the door. Our brand is our strength and excellence needs to come as standard.

'The culture is built and underpinned within the organisation by rewarding the behaviours and practices they are seeking to see more of. When I worked at IBM we had quarterly customer success rewards in my area. When we issued the rewards we linked them to the practice, hence encouraging more of the behaviour that supports the practice. We really want to encourage people to do the right thing.

'The practices were developed using crowd sourcing. Everyone at IBM could contribute their ideas on what they felt was important to the purpose, values and practices. This was curated and distilled into the 1-3-9. They have 1 purpose, 3 values and 9 practices. The purpose is "To Be Essential".

'This refers to how IBM can touch many lives without them necessarily even knowing it is there. For example, IBM is working on a project which is around cancer diagnosis. People wouldn't necessarily know that IBM is part of that project. IBM is also collaborating with Nationwide Building Society with its app, but that's not obvious.

'"Be Essential" is a global statement. It's how IBM wants to be perceived. The three values it has are: dedication to every client's success, innovation that matters and trust and personal responsibility in all relationships. What makes them more specific are the practices that it uses at a more day-to-day level. Each value has three practices below them. As these were created by IBMers there is a huge amount of buy-in.

'You need to think about the value you bring to the customer. To be trusted isn't just the company name and title on your business card—it's how you demonstrate that value to the customer or client. I was fortunate in many ways; I could be trusted by the customer because of the resources that I could bring to bear. They saw the value in me because I could bring other members of my team who could solve their problems. To excel in the consulting world it requires a mixture of technical skills, industry experience and behavioural/people skills. If the people skills or behavioural skills are missing there will always be a problem because the consultant cannot truly build trust with the client. There are a couple of exceptions I have seen over the years in the industry, where the individual might be so technically competent that their lack of people skills are overlooked, but it is very rare.'

Dominic Myles was working for IBM at the time of the interview. He has since moved on in his career.

Client expectations of a low-cost organisation

For contrast, we then interviewed Tony Davis, former CEO of Bmibaby Ltd. This was a low-cost airline. 'We wanted our customers to get off their flight saying, "That was better than I expected." We never expected them to say, "That was amazing." Delivering against our core values of price, punctuality, and low numbers of suitcases lost was how we measured our success. Our customers were clear on this when we sold them the product.

'You have to be transparent—do what it says on the tin. Many airlines over promise and under deliver and try and create a perception that isn't reality. It's important not to over promise when fares are low. You must demonstrate value for money. If you are charging a premium price you have to have either tremendous service or products or both.

'The management has to drive the culture in order for the customer to trust the organisation. There is no point in offering low fares and then saying you're better than your competition—you will come unstuck and not be able to deliver on your promise. Candour is important.

'Under delivering is an inherent problem for senior managers. The disconnect between the marketers and the customer experience can be huge. Delivering against the core values of the business is important. When the customer doesn't get what they're expecting, they have no loyalty. This is relevant at all points of access. If it was easier to book, a flight should then be punctual, easy to board and the bag should be at the other end. The customer is buying the organisation, not just one part of it.'

Measuring behaviour

A strong performance framework will clearly identify both the operational and behavioural skills required to meet your organisation's objectives. All team members should be in no doubt about their core role, how to carry out this role and how this role contributes to the business's purpose, mission and vision.

It is imperative to have a performance framework that supports a service vision. A tick-box exercise in itself is not enough. Some organisations believe they have a strong framework in place, when in reality the performance criteria are just statements—there is no clear evidence that these statements are being carried out. It's not what you do; it's how you do it. We're sure you can think of a time when you received service that was technically fine but that left you feeling unvalued as a client!

Does your organisation's performance include positive behaviours that will impact on client satisfaction?

Client satisfaction

Consistency at every touchpoint in the client journey is vital. Any weak links in this journey will damage your credibility as a whole. Make it a habit to check in with your clients throughout the process.

Often, organisations view client satisfaction as a form-filling exercise at the end of a sales process. A face-to-face interaction with your client to gain an understanding of his or her experience throughout the process will be more valuable to your organisation.

At the end of a transaction, consider asking this simple question: '**Would you wholeheartedly recommend our**

business to a friend?' The answer will tell you much of what you need to know. And if you ask this question while face-to-face with your client, you will be able to delve deeper and ask more questions, to understand more specifically what made the service legendary or what needs to be improved.

'Client satisfaction is an intangible asset to your business.' – © *First Impressions Training*

Jeff Bezos, CEO of Amazon, places high value on client-satisfaction ratings in his business. He uses the concept of 'the empty chair'. During meetings, he asks his managers to answer to the empty chair in the room, which is deemed to be Amazon's best customer. The empty chair is the ultimate boss at Amazon!

Who in your organisation demonstrates a high level of service aptitude and builds great relationships?

Could these people be used as champions in the business to model great behaviour?

Rewarding behaviour

Rewards should acknowledge great behaviour and not solely performance (e.g., hitting sales targets). Rewarding achievement alone could lead to unscrupulous behaviour at the cost of building great relationships.

We recommend rewarding behaviour that has a team focus rather than an individual focus. For example, if there is a standard that incoming calls should be answered within five rings, meeting this standard could be a collective team effort, not an individual's role. A specific group target like this encourages more collaborative working and clearly indicates desired behaviours.

Positive behaviour costs nothing, and the value it adds to the organisation is priceless and often intangible. We only need to look back to Enron and Lehman Brothers to see examples of behaviour driven by personal gain. Rewards should not be divisive, but sadly they often are.

Pentlands Accountants & Business Advisors set a great example. Their rewards are both collaborative and driven by a focus on doing the right thing for their clients. Managing director Elinor Perry told us about their monthly 'Shining Star' award. 'The award was originally presented to the team members who had given great service and demonstrated our values.

'Over time it has evolved, and the current holder of the award nominates the winner, stating the reason for the nomination. We have a presentation in the office and the winner keeps the award on their desk for the month. We also share a photo publicly on social media so our clients can see too.

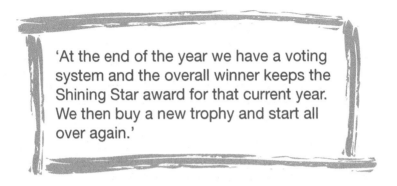

'At the end of the year we have a voting system and the overall winner keeps the Shining Star award for that current year. We then buy a new trophy and start all over again.'

We love this idea—it encourages positive behaviour and it's a team-driven initiative. The process is also fair, as the same person can't win twice in a row.

What do you do to reward great behaviour in your organisation?

Service recovery

Of course mistakes will happen in all businesses. Systems can fail and human error can creep in. Excellent organisations recognise this and have processes in place to resolve problems in a way that exceeds clients' expectations. Ultimately, the client should not remember the original problem but what was done to put it right.

We saw a great example of this recently while delivering service excellence training within a professional services business.

After her bank made an error, our client was unable to use her credit card, and her account was suspended. The bank corrected the error speedily. Shortly afterward, she got married, and was surprised to receive a wedding hamper from the bank. Two years later she had a baby, and received a baby hamper! She was so blown away, she could hardly remember what the bank had done wrong in the first place. Instead, she spent most of her time telling us how great the organisation was and what they had done to resolve the situation.

She has probably shared this story countless times—and this is great marketing for the bank. If they had not taken this service-recovery action, she could have been sharing the negative story, rather than the positive one.

When mistakes are made in your organisation, look at what went wrong with the process and reflect on the behaviour that was demonstrated. How could you improve both the processes and the behaviours?

Complaints are often described as opportunities. But they are only opportunities if you resolve them in a way that further cements the relationship with your client and demonstrates outstanding service-aptitude skills.

Behaviour in communication

You might read this next section and think the information seems obvious. We would agree. But we are constantly surprised to find that basic standards are not always in place, so we will cover them in brief. As you read, ask yourself, 'Are these standards being met in my organisation?'

'If you are not fulfilling the basic standards, you don't truly know them.'
– © *First Impressions Training*

In today's digitised world, organisations must be aware of the entire client journey to ensure consistency across all communication channels.

It is important that all communication—written, digital and face-to-face—is consistent with the organisation's brand message and non-negotiable standards in terms of behaviour.

Team members should be encouraged to give feedback when they spot great behaviour, and also when they spot behaviour that could be improved upon, to keep the standards high.

Meeting management

We have all been to meetings that are a complete waste of time. Following a few simple guidelines will ensure that meetings are useful and productive.

◊ Attend a meeting only if you know that you can add value.
◊ Be prepared—what are your desired outcomes?
◊ Take great notes.
◊ Be punctual.
◊ Understand the protocol—is it a formal or more relaxed meeting?
◊ Dress appropriately—see *Element 5: Professional image—Dress codes.*
◊ Have a strong agenda.
◊ Contribute well to the meeting. Think about your mindset, your communication style, your interaction and your behaviour.
◊ Make sure your points are heard but don't frequently interrupt.
◊ Ask questions as the meeting progresses—don't save them all until the end.
◊ Be a good listener.
◊ Avoid being a distraction, e.g., fiddling with pens, tapping fingers or rustling papers.
◊ Always keep your phone on silent—interruptions can damage the flow of the meeting.
◊ Remain calm and professional.
◊ Avoid secondary conversations (this is very disrespectful).
◊ Keep the confidential elements of the meeting confidential.
◊ Be respectful of the chair even if he or she is less senior.

◊ Be aware of where you are sitting and the impact this can have. Ensure you are visible to all participants; otherwise, you may be forgotten.

◊ Consider the meeting room's layout and environment— this can have a bearing on how attendees feel.

Meeting participants will make decisions based on what they see from you in the meeting. They will hold these perceptions long after the meeting ends. Did they see confidence, contribution, good articulation, appropriate gestures, an ability to engage in healthy conflict and a commitment to carrying out actions and being accountable?

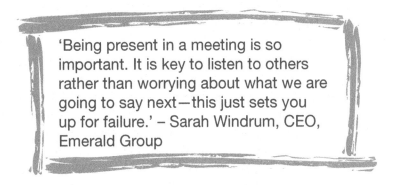

'Being present in a meeting is so important. It is key to listen to others rather than worrying about what we are going to say next—this just sets you up for failure.' – Sarah Windrum, CEO, Emerald Group

Email

Many people state that email is their preferred way of communicating. Because email can be sent from so many different devices, the etiquette of business communication can easily be lost. Keep the following points in mind when emailing business contacts.

◊ Ensure the tone matches the type of message being communicated.

◊ Avoid text language; e.g., 'l8r' (later), 'lol' (laugh out loud), 'ur' (you are).

◊ Make sure text colour is appropriate—black is most formal, albeit you may wish to use your brand colour to differentiate.

◊ Ensure the title of the email is relevant to the subject.

◊ Do not say it's urgent if it's not.

◊ Use correct grammar and spelling.

◊ Avoid copying everyone in replies in an attempt to cover your back.

◊ Think twice before emailing someone who sits across the office—consider whether human interaction would be more effective.

◊ Separate emails concerning different subjects to avoid long emails.

◊ Be aware of emojis—these can be used to good effect with friends, but in many sectors they are seen as unprofessional.

◊ Avoid writing anything in an email that you would not want to see as public property.

◊ Be mindful of what is in the email footer—if it's too long, nobody will read it.

◊ Be consistent with company branding.

◊ Consider using your photograph in the footer to help build a human connection.

◊ Avoid writing in capitals—it can come across as shouting and being agressive.

◊ Consider how you represent yourself in email format—is it different to how you show up in person?

◊ Ask yourself if it would be more productive to pick up the phone rather than engage in email tennis.

Texting and mobile phones

Most people will have a company phone, a personal phone, or both. Having standards for their use is advisable.

◊ Texting is more common than calling these days. But you must be aware of where the focus lies: are employees checking phones and texting in the presence of clients, prospects or colleagues? If someone is glued to a device, the focus is clearly not on the other people in the room.

◊ Implement a no-out-of-hours-texting policy (unless there is an absolute emergency). It is important for staff to have downtime to recharge their batteries, and they can't do so if they receive constant interruptions.

◊ Phones should be switched off or on silent during meetings and conferences, to prevent distractions. If a phone does ring, the person receiving the call should either cancel it or take it outside the room. It's always worth checking to make sure your phone is on silent, to avoid embarrassment.

◊ Speaking of phones ringing, what about those ring tones? Ensure that you are not going to be embarrassed by your ring tone if your phone does happen to go off.

◊ If an urgent call is expected during a meeting, let people know. This should only happen in cases where there are emgerencies, not regularly.

◊ Ensure answerphone messages are appropriate for a business setting. They should be short and to the point, and they should be consistent with the company's brand.

◊ If you are in a meeting with prospects and clients, keep phones away from the meeting table. It is all too easy to compulsively pick up your phone if it is within reach.

◊ When in public, use your phone with caution. How often have you overheard conversations on a train and been surprised by the content? People often seem to be unaware of how much can be gleaned from a one-sided conversation.

Social and business networks

Business networking sites

Some social networking sites are designed primarily for business use rather than personal. LinkedIn is the most popular business networking site right now. At the time of writing, LinkedIn had over 300 million members in over 200 countries around the globe.

Ensure that your profile is professional and that it reflects both your individual brand and the brand of the organisation you work for.

Things to consider

◊ Make sure you have a photograph and that it is professional—a snap from a wedding or a party won't do!
◊ Complete your profile; otherwise, you may miss opportunities.
◊ Be mindful of your writing style. Ensure that it is consistent with the company's brand personality.
◊ Use LinkedIn as part of your strategy for building trusted relationships—do not use it as purely a place to sell, or get a new job.
◊ Consider the frequency of your updates: do not bombard contacts with serial updates!
◊ Keep personal and business profiles separate.

◊ Connect with people with whom you could develop a business relationship. A small list of engaged contacts is better than a huge list with no engagement.

Many companies have business pages on sites such as Facebook and Twitter. The organisation should have a clear policy on how these are managed and who can post on the company page. Once a post is published, it can go viral very quickly—and the organisation will then lose control of it. This is particularly true if the issue is sensitive and emotive.

Donna's story   The managing partner of a national accountancy firm contacted us regarding a middle manager's LinkedIn profile. The picture was 'provocative and inappropriate'. He was concerned about how to handle the situation, as a personal LinkedIn profile is currently employee-owned data, rather than a company tool. This is becoming a real concern for many HR teams within organisations. We advised the company to set clear non-negotiable standards for social media usage. This is imperative if you want to avoid these types of situations.

How to lose clients with just a few tweets

In 2016, a law firm who acts for local authorities triggered anger amongst parents of children with disabilities following posts on social media. The founder sent out a tirade of gloating tweets after winning a case against a family whose child had severe disabilites.

The messages unleashed a backlash of complaints from outraged parents and the general public. The tweets were deleted within hours; however, thousands of people had already shared them. The damage to the organisation had been done, and their apology, released along with a promise to donate to a children's charity, was seen as insignificant. No amount of money would put this right. Within 48 hours the law firm had lost 8 out of 20 contracts with the local authorities they acted for. A very expensive mistake and untold damage to the company's reputation!

Social networking sites

Privacy settings should be locked down so that only friends or connections can see updates. Most recruiting managers will check applicant profiles on social media.

◊ Profile pictures are generally visible to all, so be careful. You may not want your team members posting photos of themselves in their swimwear or with a glass of their favourite tipple in hand!

◊ Both Facebook and Twitter have a business account option. Ensure that the business page is kept for business communication and not for personal use.

◊ Make a conscious decision about whom to add as a connection on personal sites. For example, what would you do if a business contact sent a request to be friends on Facebook? Having clear standards as an organisation can be helpful for employees, and prevent unnecessary embarrassment. We recommend saving Facebook for family and friends, and requesting that business contacts connect with you on LinkedIn, Twitter and business Facebook pages.

◊ Dashboard applications such as Tweetdeck allow posts to be sent out to all social media sites at once. We would not advise this, as each social media platform has slightly different uses and slightly different audiences. It is much better to customise the message to fit the audience being communicated with. Statistics show that messages sent directly from a platform receive much more engagement than those sent from a social media dashboard.

'In the digital age, even when you are not working, you are working. Be consistent with your networks across all media.'

In fact, we saw a great example of inconsistent social media behaviour recently. An acquaintance we thought was credible and professional completely dented her credibility through her behaviour on social media. We actually agreed with her sentiment, but the way she presented her view was totally unprofessional, and it has made us think twice about associating with her.

Lyn's story   When I was a professional services manager, I was looking to recruit a consultant who was in a strong position to get the job. I checked social media, and the candidate had just posted on a social site, saying, 'Can't wait to head off travelling in the summer.' Needless to say, this individual did not get the job!

What is your policy on social media?

Social behaviour

Corporate hospitality, although not as popular as it was in the hedonistic 80s, is still a requirement for many client services team members. It is important to remember that you are still on company business, not on a night out with friends.

Ensure that team members conduct themselves appropriately and avoid overindulging, so they do not embarrass themselves or the client.

Do you have a clear policy on social behaviour?

Habits detrimental to building relationships

A habit is a behaviour that is repeated regularly and often unconsciously. Be aware of habits that could prevent professional-relationship building and identify habits that could enhance it. We often see poor behaviour—such as inappropriate humour, bad language and overuse of phones or computers in meetings—allowed to pass unchallenged. You should model good habits, and give feedback if people are displaying negative or irritating habits (for example, people often lean back on their chairs and lift the front two legs off the floor. This may be comfortable, but it looks disrespectful and conveys boredom).

'We are what we repeatedly do. Excellence then is not an act but a habit.' – Aristotle

Brand sabotage

The digitised world offers great advantages, but it also provides a platform for unhappy clients to damage your brand via social media or your website. Previously, clients might have complained to friends and family. Now, they can share a complaint worldwide with the click of a button.

In a client's eyes, your organisation is a single entity, so if she receives different standards of service from different individuals, then her experience is diminished and the organisation's credibility is reduced and its reputation is tarnished.

And if the culture isn't good within an organisation, some staff may become brand saboteurs. Here are some classic examples of brand sabotage:

◊ refusal to take responsibility for client concerns ('It's not my job!')
◊ blaming another part of the business
◊ blaming the management
◊ not believing in the service
◊ interdepartment disparity (unwillingness to support colleagues in other departments)
◊ gossip, and
◊ disconnection between the brand and the experience.

Say one of the organisation's values is being caring, but a client then deals with a staff member who is apathetic and unwilling to help. There is a clear conflict, and the brand's values are being sabotaged. We see and hear examples of this conflict happening constantly in meetings, emails and phone calls and during networking events.

 Where in your organisation do you see or hear of this happening?

Removing barriers

Some organisations build their processes around challenging clients, but this puts barriers in place, making it difficult for the majority of clients to access services, rather than just the minority. It is better to build processes for the 95% majority, rather than the 5% minority.

 Are there any negative practices in place in your organisation?

What we refer to as 'Coffeegate' is an example of introducing a negative practice for the minority.

Coffeegate

While working with a professional service client, we overheard a conversation about building a process to stop clients from coming in and having free coffee when they are not there for a substantial business reason.

The reality is that these clients are in the minority. It will cost only a few extra pounds per week to give drinks to the small number of clients who take advantage of this benefit. Why establish a whole process to figure out the reason for the visit just to determine whether to offer the client a coffee or not? The positive feeling gained by the satisfied, coffee-drinking client will increase the company's reputation through word-of-mouth marketing.

 In your workbook you will find a self-audit. Check how you score on behavioural skills.

www.firstimpressions.uk.com/trusted/

Mastering the art of great behaviour is a key component to building trust. Getting it wrong can really damage your credibility; getting it right can take you one step closer to finding your T-Spot.

Credibility sleuth

- Ensure leaders model the desired behaviours.

- Set non-negotiable standards that everyone is expected to operate within.

- Do the right thing—it will create a ripple effect of kindness, and a feel-good factor.

- Measure behaviour through a strong performance framework, focusing on HOW employees carry out their role.

- Acknowledge and reward great behaviour and outstanding relationships.

- Surprise and delight your clients when they complain.

- Be aware of proper etiquette and expected behaviour in all forms of communication.

- Ensure behaviour is consistent. In the eyes of your client, the organisation is a single entity.

- Build processes for the 95% majority, not the 5% minority.

 Credibility thief

- A command-and-control culture will not bring out the best in the employees.

- Without standards, both internal and external relationships will be left to chance.

- Following processes without considering the human approach is potentially damaging to the client experience.

- A process and sales driven performance framework will impact negatively on client-satisfaction ratings.

- Rewards should not be divisive and should not encourage unscrupulous behaviour.

- Clients who complain should not be seen as difficult clients— they are actually helping you to improve and grow your business.

- Having no etiquette policies or standards of behaviour for communication is a risk to achieving consistency of service.

- A blame culture will damage your brand.

- Negative barriers make it difficult for your clients to do business with you.

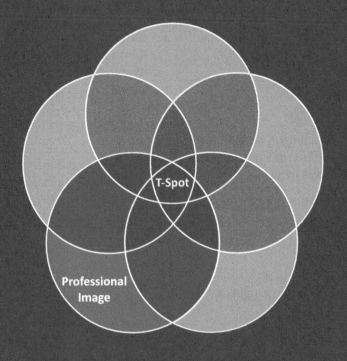

'You have no control over
how others perceive you, but
you can control what you are
communicating.'

Many companies overlook the concept of professional image. In our experience, this is because they are unsure of how best to tackle it. Fear or apathy prevents them from guiding their teams, so people are left to their own devices. Some organisations, however, go the opposite way and enforce a regimented dress-code policy that makes everyone feel restricted. Standards for dress are essential to ensure the organisation's brand is consistent and professional.

Professional image

'There is a happy medium that will take account of people's differences, allowing them to be their authentic selves and ensuring that the dress code is appropriate for the company too.'

What we wear can make us feel more confident

How we dress not only affects how others perceive us—it also greatly affects how we perceive ourselves. Dressing with confidence and knowing we look good has a knock-on effect on how we feel. It improves our self-worth and self-image, and in turn, this impacts on the relationships we build. The clothes you wear don't just change the way you see yourself; wearing certain kinds of clothes can affect your behaviour and change the way you think.

This is a topic now attracting more research. Psychologists call it 'enclothed cognition'. The studies in this area so far have been small, but the outcome of all of them is that the clothes we wear affect our thinking and can improve performance.

Hajo Adam and Adam Galinsky carried out critical trials to test enclothed cognition. In the first trial, participants were asked to carry out a Stroop test: identify the colour of ink words are written in while ignoring the written words themselves (e.g., 'green' written in red ink).

Participants were split into two groups. The first group wore lab coats, and the second wore their own clothes. The first made half as many errors as the second. A lab coat is synonymous with attention to detail and accuracy.

In the second trial, the students carried out a Stroop test while wearing white coats. Half were told they were wearing doctors' coats, while half were told they were wearing painters' coats. Those wearing the 'doctors' coats' showed sustained attention. The current research suggests that the wearer's psychological processes are affected by the symbolic meaning and the physical wearing of the clothes.

According to Dr Galinsky, 'Clothes can have profound and systematic psychological and behavioural consequences for their wearers. Clothes invade the body and brain, putting the wearer into a different psychological state.'

The British Psychological Society suggests that future research could examine the effects of other types of clothing. Might the robes of a priest make us more moral? Might a firefighter's suit make us braver? Adam and Galinsky concluded: 'Although the saying goes that "clothes do not make the man", our results suggest that they do hold a strange power over their wearers.'

Dr Karen Pine, professor of psychology at Hertfordshire University, conducted further research. She split her students into three groups: one group wore a Superman T-shirt, one wore a plain blue T-shirt and one wore their own clothing. A number of lab tests asked the students to rate their superiority, confidence and attractiveness. Overall, the Superman T-shirt wearers scored significantly higher, rating themselves as superior, more confident and more attractive. They even thought they could lift more weight than the other students!

How fascinating that the glib phrase 'dress for success' has more bearing on us than we might have thought.

Our clothing really does have an effect on our thought processes.

Even putting on a pair of glasses can make a difference. If you put a pair on right now, how would your posture change? How do you think people would perceive you? Do you think you would look more intelligent?

Cycle of success

Imagine how you would feel if you had a clothing malfunction at work. You would most likely want to hide away in your corner of the office and not interact with colleagues. You would therefore avoid opportunities to interact and your overall performance that day would be compromised.

By contrast, imagine how you would feel if you wore an outfit to work that you felt great in, and people complimented you on it. You would stand a little taller, your shoulders would be back a little further, you would carry yourself with confidence and you would smile more. Feeling like this, you would be happy to interact with colleagues and your performance that day would be greatly improved.

In short, this is known as the cycle of success.

© First Impressions Training

People judge us by what we wear

In a business context, people judge us all the time. You may not like this, but it is a fact of life. Once we accept this, we can choose how to react.

Lyn's story   When I managed a group of consultants and project managers, I would ask them to consider the impression they made when they first met their clients. 'Would a client believe that you're worth your day rate? If not, you'll be on your back foot all day and will have to work harder to prove yourself. If you do meet their expectations, the client won't question it, you'll make a better impression and you'll find your job easier to do.'

How we dress is not the only thing we are judged on, of course, but because it's one of the first things people have to go on in terms of decision-making, it's an important one. Presenting yourself well will help demonstrate your competence.

Why do people judge us? It goes back to our inbuilt fight-or-flight response. We are ultimately trying to decide 'Is this person a friend or foe?' Of course we don't need to run away from woolly mammoths these days, but we do sometimes meet people that make us wary or, indeed, fearful.

A number of research projects have proved this. But that aside, how often have you felt either overdressed or underdressed for an occasion? Most of us will experience this at some point in our career and will have a story to tell. And when this happens, we are unable to perform at our best.

Client story   'I was on my way to a really important prospect meeting in London. I bent down to pick up my briefcase and my trousers ripped all along the back seam! I quickly went into the nearest clothes shop and bought a pair of trousers that matched my suit jacket as closely as possible. I went off to the meeting, but was conscious all day that my jacket and trousers did not match. I'm sure this impeded my performance that day, and I know that I was unable to be totally focused. This highlighted the importance of what we wear and the psychological effect our clothes can have upon us.'

Just as you would prepare for a meeting in terms of your notes, your presentation and your desired outcomes, it's equally important to prepare your image and consider the impact you wish to make. Take a planned approach to your working wardrobe.

Choose your outfit each day based on the following considerations:

◊ how you want to feel
◊ the image you wish to portray
◊ the culture of your organisation (though it's important to be authentic as well)
◊ whether you wish to blend in or stand out
◊ how much authority you need to display
◊ the type of clients you are meeting and the appropriate dress code
◊ the messages you wish to send out
◊ any environmental considerations, and
◊ the 'team look'.

We will address this in more detail in the following pages.

How do you want to show up?

Do you want to stand out as the expert and lead the meeting or interaction, or are you a participant who wants to blend in?

Reflecting the culture of your organisation while remaining authentic

It's important to consider your organisation's culture and brand values and how they can be linked to the way you represent yourself through your image. For example, if you work for a technology company such as Facebook or Google, it's perfectly acceptable to wear casual clothing.

Imagine you have a meeting with someone from Facebook or Google and she arrives at the meeting in a pinstriped suit. This probably wouldn't sit comfortably with you. It would be incongruent with the company's brand and would cause you to question her authenticity. In turn, this would cause you to question whether you could trust the organisation.

Equally, we are sure you would be surprised if your solicitor arrived at a meeting wearing jeans and a hoodie!

Of course we all have our own preferences when it comes to how we present ourselves, and we can weave these in while still conforming to a corporate image. Remember when you had to wear a school uniform? There were always those who managed to personalise it to show their personality and individuality. Now, we are not condoning rolling up your skirt or pulling threads out of your tie, but there are ways of personalising your image even when a uniform or dress code must be adhered to.

For example, if you work in a highly corporate environment but prefer a creative style of dress, you could wear the required business suit but add accessories—e.g., a pocket square with more pattern and colour—or design features, such as coloured thread for the button holes (think Paul Smith).

What is the culture of your organisation and how can you reinforce it through your personal brand image?

Personal style: Blending in or standing out

Our clothing choices are influenced by our physical characteristics, colouring and lifestyle. Our personal style is determined by our personality.

There are five typical style personality types, and style personality is, to a large extent, unisex. While the likes, dislikes, habits and preferences will be broadly similar for men and women, there are a few minor differences (e.g., approach to jewellery, accessories and make-up).

Your personality has a profound effect on the way you choose to dress and present yourself. You create your personal style by wearing clothes and accessories that reflect your individual personality. When you feel and look comfortable in your clothes, you give off an air of self-assurance and ensure that you (and not just your clothes) get noticed.

Most people have one predominant style personality but can have elements of two or three. Identifying the key characteristics of your preferred style personality can help you understand why you prefer a certain look, or feel more comfortable in certain types of clothes. Knowing this, you can work with your preferences rather than try to conform to a style that is not naturally yours.

Understanding your style personality will also enhance your confidence. If you feel right, you will perform better.

The five style personality types are as follows.

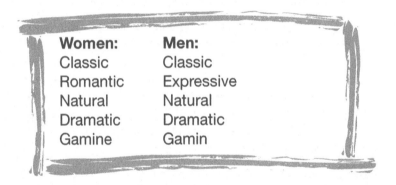

Women:	Men:
Classic	Classic
Romantic	Expressive
Natural	Natural
Dramatic	Dramatic
Gamine	Gamin

The five personalities

Here is a brief overview of each style personality.

Classic: co-ordinated, elegant, timeless, well cut; generally prefers neutrals and avoids bright colours; often needs help with casual dressing, as he or she prefers to be smartly and formally dressed.

Romantic/Expressive: creative, artistic, sensuous; likes accessories and clothes that feel good against the skin (e.g., cashmere); often needs help ensuring a professional look (accessories, make-up and fabrics can be overdone) with a nod to personality preferences.

Natural: relaxed, comfortable, easy to wear, simple; generally doesn't like shopping for clothes and rarely, if ever, wears cosmetics; often needs to pay particular attention to grooming.

Dramatic: bold, strong, adventurous, individual; likes to make a statement; needs help not overdoing it in a business context.

Gamin/Gamine: youthful, sporty, neat, co-ordinated, quirky; can sometimes dress in a manner that is too youthful, which can damage credibility.

We strongly advocate bringing your personality into your outfit choice. For business, ensure that your overall image balances the brand of the organisation you represent and your own personal style. A compromise can often be reached. For example, Theresa May demonstrates her dramatic style through her choice of footwear while maintaining a professional, polished image.

 In your workbook you will find an exercise to help you establish which style personality reflects your preferences. **www.firstimpressions.uk.com/trusted/**

How much authority you need to display

Think about occupations that require authority. Police, judges and security guards wear clothing with colours that starkly contrast (e.g., black with white). This contrast demonstrates authority—it is ingrained in our society.

To create your most authoritative look, aim for maximum contrast of colour to suit your natural colour pattern. Also, consider the formality of your clothing. The more formal the clothing, the more authoritative you will appear. (See *Dress codes*.) As mentioned, black with white is a strong contrast, but many other combinations will achieve the same effect without appearing severe. For example, a smart dark suit worn with a white or pale pastel shirt will automatically show authority. If you wish to appear more approachable, wear outfits with less contrast.

Let's assume you have a mentoring session with one of your team members. It's better to appear approachable in these circumstances, rather than authoritative. To project a more approachable appearance, consider wearing the following:

◊ Softer fabrics (e.g., wool)
◊ Colours or patterns
◊ Different shades of the same colour; medium to low contrast
◊ Separates
◊ No formal items (e.g., business jackets or ties)

The type of clients you are meeting

Lyn's story When I was a project manager I worked with various clients. I remember one week working with Harley-Davidson one day and a City bank the next. As you can imagine, at Harley everyone is fairly casual, and staff dress in branded Harley clothing. I would have stood out like a sore thumb in a formal business suit! I still wanted to project a professional image though, so I relaxed my dress code slightly by opting for separates. I wore a coloured jacket, a top with no collar and black trousers. This suited the client environment and ensured that I built trust and empathy with the client. Of course a line must be drawn—I wouldn't have gone dressed in jeans and biker gear, but very formal attire could have created a barrier.

How can you express your individuality while still dressing appropriately for the sector you work within?

What is appropriate for different situations?

We can group occasions and appropriate styles of clothing into categories or levels of dress:

- Formal business
- Relaxed business
- Business casual
- Tidy casual

Dress codes

Understanding these style categories can help you create an appropriate look for every occasion.

Formal Business
- Matched suits
- Plain fabrics
- Formal shirt/blouse
- Darkest colours
- High contrast

Relaxed Business
- Lighter colours or unmatched suits
- Texture or subtle patterns on suits
- Less contrast
- Less formal shirt/blouse

Business Casual
- Less formal but co-ordinated styles
- Separates
- Relaxed designs or fabrics
- Brighter/lighter colours

Tidy Casual
- No jacket
- Unstructured styles
- Fun colours/styles
- Patterns

This is an area that many companies pay little or no attention to. Giving it even a small amount of consideration can positively affect client relationships in a big way.

Many of our clients have reported back on how useful it is for both individuals and the organisation as a whole to understand the impact of professional image.

Creative agency story   In this industry, 'chemistry meetings' with prospects are common—meetings to determine whether they will work well together. The team now discusses how they will dress for the meetings. If the client is very formal in their dress, they will also dress in formal business attire but with a creative twist to demonstrate their design-led philosophy.

Management consultancy story   A client of ours was working with a mental health hospital. The client was concerned that showing up in suits might have a negative effect on the patients, even though the meeting was with the hospital's management team. So they removed their jackets and ties to create a more relaxed image. While remaining professional, they also considered the needs of the patients in the hospital setting.

A small tweak to what we wear can have a huge impact on the relationships we build and the trust we engender.

Digital agency story   What to wear when meeting both a prominent MP and the head of digital for a political party? Our client, a digital agency, opted for a smart casual look: shirts, tailored trousers and tailored jackets. In digital departments, the dress code is generally jeans and a T-shirt, but as they were also meeting an MP, they decided to smarten up a little.

When they were introduced to the MP, she immediately tore into them for having the audacity to turn up for a meeting with her not wearing a suit! She explained that it was an honour for them to have the opportunity to work with the party and they were clearly not taking it seriously.

They went along to the meeting room and shortly afterwards, a young man came into the room wearing jeans, T-shirt and trainers. The MP rounded on him and said, 'We have this room booked for a meeting with the head of digital.' You guessed it—he was the head of digital! She then bombarded him with a flurry of questions about his age (23), how long he had worked there (since university) and what he had done prior to being in his current role. Interrogation over, they were able to proceed with the meeting. She followed up with an email urging all of them to buy decent suits.

A while later, this same MP was heard on the radio complaining that women were under the microscope for their clothing rather than their policies. The words 'pot', 'kettle' and 'black' sprang to mind!

When dress-code expectations are not met, the other person can see it as a sign of disrespect.

Lyn's story A male colleague and I were going to a pitch meeting at an auction house to implement a new planning solution for them. We had previously decided that our company style was relaxed business. The men would wear suits with patterned (checked or striped) shirts and no ties. We arrived and the prospects were male, all wearing ties. And not only ties—branded auction house ties! At the end of the pitch, the prospect turned to my male colleague and said, 'We really like what you have shown us, but next time you come to visit us, please wear a tie!'

Fortunately, we had enough going for us in other aspects of the T-Spot Model that we got away with it. We did go back.

My colleague did wear a tie. And we won the work! If other aspects of the model had not been present, it could easily have been a very different story.

Breaking the rules completely is a no-no, but research in the *Journal of Consumer Research* suggests that deviating slightly from dress codes is advantageous. This is due to the assumption that those people who do are powerful enough to risk the social cost of such behaviour.

Business casual

This is something we are asked about frequently. Gone are the days when everyone wore suits in offices. Today, professional dress codes are a minefield. Dressing down does not automatically mean casual. It simply means less formal than traditional business wear. You need to strike the balance between being comfortable and being taken seriously. Co-ordination is key; pay attention to tone, colour and fabric weight—this is vital if you want your more casual look to create the professional impact you want. Clothes should be clean and well maintained. Accessories, such as pens, bags and jewellery that are business-like, are important to complete the look. And shoes are usually what make the big difference between a truly casual look and a more business-like one.

Business casual dos and don'ts

Do wear:

◊ shirts or blouses in plain colours or subtle patterns
◊ button-down, polo or V-neck shirts (these work best for men)
◊ fine-gauge knitwear in plain colours
◊ smart chinos or relaxed trousers in neutral colours
◊ structured fabrics and styles, or
◊ jackets in contemporary colours.

Don't wear:

◊ scruffy jeans or scruffy T-shirts
◊ chunky or multicoloured knitwear
◊ colours that don't work together (or too many different colours)
◊ inappropriate accessories (too dressy or too casual)
◊ tatty bags or shoes, or
◊ anything from your evening or holiday wardrobe.

Dress-down Friday

Many companies have adopted a 'dress-down Friday' policy. But consider enclothed cognition—the effect our clothes have on our behaviour. It is worth thinking through the implications of casual dress.

Lyn's story When delivering programmes for a national utilities company, I was working with women returning to work after having children. We were talking about the days they worked, and they all seemed to work Fridays. I casually remarked that when I went back to work part-time after having my daughter, I liked having a long weekend off. They all said they liked working on Friday because it was a dress-down day and they all went to the pub and little work got done. I cringe thinking about the loss of productivity due to this initiative!

Some organisations state that they use relaxed dress codes as a reward or to boost morale and improve communication internally. The issue of whether dress code affects productivity is unclear. Productivity isn't driven purely by dress code; there are several factors at play. Company culture and client expectations in the sector need to be considered too.

A dress-down Friday policy certainly requires clear guidelines to ensure professional relationships are maintained.

Tips for dress-down Friday

◊ Ensure clothing is at least at the standard of business casual (see the *Business casual* section).
◊ Consider the impression it may give clients.
◊ Think about extending the dress-down policy to visiting clients so they don't feel overdressed.
◊ Consider the impact it may have on behaviour and productivity.
◊ Think about making a regular donation to charity as part of your corporate social responsibility, to make it worthwhile.

Cultural and religious differences

Organisations should acknowledge the existence of religious and cultural diversity. Before implementing dress codes, you need to consider these differences.

Which dress codes are appropriate for your organisation and for the types of clients you work with?

The messages you wish to send out

The psychology of colour

Colour is an important aspect of the human experience. It creates both physiological and emotional responses. It's therefore natural that the colours around us and the colours we wear affect us. When you choose clothes that suit your individual physical characteristics, you will not only look your best but also feel good and get maximum value for money out of your clothes. The psychology of colour can help you align with the message you want to deliver. Think about a manager delivering a sombre message—if he or

she was dressed in fun clothing and bright colours, the
audience would receive a mixed message.

**Dressing in colours that support the
message you are aiming to portray will
strengthen communication.**

Reaction and response to colour

Meaning of colour	Things to consider
Black	
Authoritative, assertive, powerful, sophisticated, oppressive, menacing	Black is great for high authority, not good for approachability. Also, be aware of the hierarchy in your office environment. If your boss doesn't wear black, it's best to avoid it.
Blue	
Intelligent, professional, trustworthy, conservative, credible, aloof, cold	Blue is a versatile colour, as it can be authoritative or approachable depending on what else is worn with it.
Grey	
Reliable, respectable, efficient, lacking energy and confidence	Grey is a good alternative to black for business. Avoid wearing grey on its own as it can suggest a lack of energy. Avoid in a creative environment.

Brown	
Serious, respectable, supportive, empathetic, approachable, creative, dull	The old phrase 'never wear brown in town' doesn't carry as much weight as it used to. It used to be seen as a country colour reserved for fishing and shooting. Nowadays it's more acceptable, albeit very formal businesses will still see it as too informal.
White	
(When worn with black) Authoritative, assertive, powerful, intimidating (When worn on its own) Empathetic, approachable, pure, innocent, cold	White is sharp, smart and versatile, as it matches with many other business colours. Bear in mind that it's seen differently when worn on its own rather than with other colours, especially black. Refer to the section *How much authority you need to display*. In a clinical and catering environment it represents cleanliness and sterility.
Red	
Powerful, dynamic, assertive, successful, aggressive, demanding	Red is a great colour to wear if you want to stand out or appear confident (e.g., if you are presenting at or chairing a meeting). It is not advisable in an appraisal situation or an environment where you wish to instil calm.

Green	
Harmonious, approachable, empathetic, trustworthy, boring, bland	Green is good to wear in a coaching or conflict resolution situation, as it is calming. It's therefore not the best colour to wear if you are delivering a presentation, unless you opt for a bright green to draw attention.
Purple	
Creative, innovative, confident, high quality, authentic, successful, ageing	When you need to be creative and project a self-assured image, purple is the ideal colour to wear. With its link to royalty, it's a great colour for authority, especially if you wish to avoid black.
Orange	
Youthful, dynamic, fun, energetic, abundant, immature, frivolous	You may not be taken seriously if you wear orange in professional service organisations. People have reported being treated with a lack of respect when wearing orange. In a creative environment it can work very well.
Yellow	
Sunny, optimistic, friendly, approachable, cowardly	In a professional environment yellow should be used sparingly. It is a difficult colour to wear, so choosing the right shade to suit you is important. It is a high-energy colour so can be used to lift the mood and create a motivating environment. Conversely, it can suggest cowardice ('yellow-bellied').

Pink	
Youthful, empathetic, approachable, innovative, feminine, lightweight	Once known as a feminine colour, it's now worn equally by men and women and is a great approachable colour. Notice that politicians wear it when they are trying to be conciliatory!

How your clothes look

It is important to understand your body shape and how best to dress to flatter it. We have all seen people wearing clothes that don't fit them well or don't suit them. Even someone wearing an expensive business suit will not look his best if the suit is the wrong shape for his body or doesn't fit him well.

Gain an understanding of how a garment will work for you. Consider how it will perform when you are standing, sitting and bending. You should also ensure that the garment fits well.

We advocate purchasing the best-quality items you can afford. Choosing good-quality fabrics will stand you in good stead, as people can tell the difference between high- and low-quality fabrics.

Dr Karen Pine, professor of psychology, conducted the following study. She showed participants two photos, and they were told to look at each one for three seconds. The man in one photo was wearing a bespoke suit, and the man in the other was wearing an off-the-peg high-street suit. Participants rated the bespoke-suit wearer more favourably, stating that he seemed more confident, flexible and successful, and that he was a higher earner.

To learn what suits you in terms of your role, your personality, your colour pattern and your body, please visit our website.
www.firstimpressions.uk.com/trusted

Attention to detail/finishing touches

Grooming strategies

Immaculate grooming is vital if you want to look professional and credible. However well dressed you are, poor grooming can ruin your entire appearance. Once you establish good grooming habits, they will become part of your daily routine. Use a mirror to help you see yourself as others see you; try to check your appearance every day, including your hairstyle, front and back, in a full-length mirror. Clothing care is also important. Make time to check your clothes regularly.

Tattoos

Recent research by the British Sociological Society found that people who have tattoos could have more difficulty getting jobs. Many managers will not recruit someone with visible tattoos, and several companies now have policies on covering them. Of course, it depends on where the tattoos are, and on the type of job being applied for. For example, tattoos are perfectly acceptable in creative and artistic industries (music, media, fitness and fashion).

Whether we like it or not, first impressions are formed in less than a second, and we subconsciously form judgements about each other. We know at an intellectual level that people should be judged on their qualifications, experience and capability, but we instinctively form opinions based on visual impressions, and visible tattoos form part of that initial impression.

Dr Andrew R. Timming of the School of Management at the University of St Andrews carried out research on the impact of tattoos in the workplace. The findings showed that although the managers themselves were not keen on visible tattoos, they were more worried by what their clients might think.

Interestingly, in some professions tattoos are seen as desirable. Prison guards with tattoos have 'something to talk about', a way of building rapport with prisoners.

In later research, Timming focused on whether tattoos can have a positive impact. This was not proven to be true for the professional services industries, yet in certain places wanting to appeal to a young, trendy demographic (bars and skateboarding shops, for example), visibles tattoos were seen as positive.

Our view is that tattoos are a means of personal expression, and very individual. During an interview, it is always good to strike a balance between conforming and standing out and being authentic. But if you do opt for a visible tattoo, just know that it may limit your career choices, particularly if you are being interviewed by people of an older generation, who might view tattoos less favourably than those of a younger generation. We still do not envisage seeing lots of tattoos in the boardroom any time soon!

Lyn was interviewed on BBC Breakfast about this subject. You can see the interview on our website. **www.firstimpressions.uk.com/press/**

Finishing touches

Everything you wear and carry, down to the last detail, will say something about you. You are as good as your weakest link! Attention to personal detail will suggest attention to detail in other areas of your life, including your work.

Accessories

Consider your watch, pens, wallet, briefcase/portfolio and bags. All need to be of good quality, up to date and professional looking. They should complement your physical shape and size and reflect your personal style; they should also complement the image you are creating.

Shoes and hosiery (women)

Shoes should look smart and professional. Wearing medium heels can be viewed as more professional than flat or high-heeled shoes. Ultimately, it should be down to personal choice, rather than being forced by a dress code. The Equalities Act 2010 is in place to protect against discrimination. However, there is concern that this isn't being adhered to within some organisations. The House of Commons Petitions Committee and Women and Equalities Committee are currently reviewing this, following a petition regarding high heels and dress codes in business. (*High heels and workplace dress codes* – HC 291, published in January 2017.)

The report includes a quote from the College of Podiatry: 'We believe that there is a strong body of clinical evidence that significantly indicates the medical and disabling effects of wearing a high heel shoe over a prolonged amount of time.'

You must consider what is suitable and appropriate for your business image while considering your physical well-being too.

To create the right visual balance, ensure shoes are the same colour or darker than the hemline of your skirt/trousers. Hosiery needs to be plain, ladder and snag-free and appropriate for the outfit. Hosiery should be the same colour or lighter than your shoe colour—never darker.

Shoes and socks (men)

For a formal business look, wear black leather shoes; for a contemporary or business-casual look, go with shades of brown. The brown shoes with suits trend has stimulated press interest. Following a report published by the Social Mobility Commission (*Socio-Economic Diversity in Life Sciences and Investment Banking*, 2016), commission chairman Alan Milburn said 'arcane culture rules' were locking working-class candidates out of City jobs. The report referenced brown shoes, stating that in the City, brown shoes are seen as unacceptable business wear.

Socks for formal business should be plain and worn long enough to avoid a gap between sock and trousers. In a more relaxed business, this is one area where men can express their personality, choosing socks with more pattern and colour.

To see Lyn on BBC Breakfast speaking about the report, please visit our website.
www.firstimpressions.uk.com/press/

Jewellery

In formal business environments, jewellery needs to be low-key, professional looking, of good quality, appropriate for your bone structure and up to date.

Avoid dangling earrings and jingly bracelets, as these may be distracting. You should also avoid large signet rings and chunky bracelets, necklaces and earrings in the workplace. Cufflinks are an important accessory for men; they can be used to show your personality and individuality.

Make-up

Make-up, if worn, should be applied with care and must not be too heavy in a formal environment.

Your make-up needs to be in harmony with your natural colouring.

The devil is in the detail—what could you pay more attention to in respect of your grooming and finishing touches?

Environmental considerations

Of course there will be times where specific conditions dictate what needs to be worn. For example, one of our clients audits out on an oil rig, so the usual rules on dressing for clients do not apply. Clearly there is a health and safety consideration to take into account in this case.

Considering the 'team look'

Within professional services it is common for teams to go out on client visits (e.g., teams of management consultants, accountants, lawyers or auditors). When this happens, it is really important to consider the look of the whole team. Aim to project a consistent company image while retaining individuality. It would be good practice to double-check that everyone is meeting the required standard. Do tell your colleagues if their shirts are untucked or their laces are undone or if they have dandruff on their shoulder prior to going into a meeting. After all, it is a team effort.

The collective 'team look' is vital in building trust with colleagues, prospects and clients

It can be difficult to establish who the senior team members are if they aren't dressing for their level of seniority, especially if other team members have clearly heard the phrase 'dress for the job you want rather than the job you have'. This can cause confusion for colleagues, prospects and clients, undermine the senior managers' credibility and affect team dynamics.

Summary: Professional image

We have covered a huge amount of material in this section. There is far more to business image than people often realise. Not only do many organisations shy away from tackling this, but also, many employees don't ask for support despite the fact this is a key area of personal and professional development that the company also benefits from.

A company that invests in training in this area will reap the rewards by having confident, engaged staff members who represent the company's brand while valuing difference and individuality. More self-awareness in this area will help you discover your 1% marginal gains easily.

Dealing with employees who do not meet the dress requirement can be a headache for employers. Interpreting the current laws around dress codes can also be problematic.

Law firm Band Hatton Button LLP provides some guidance: 'Employers need to ensure that their dress code is applied even-handedly between men and women, and employers should be ready to consider exceptions where it is requested by employees who feel disadvantaged because of a protected characteristic such as sex, disability or religious belief.'

Employers who have had difficulty in this area have approached us for guidance on how to handle either organisational or individual dress-code issues. When this is handled with professionalism and sensitivity it becomes a great learning experience for the organisation, and employees will learn a new life skill too.

CASE STUDY
Aligning personal brand with corporate brand

OEE Consulting is an operations design and implementation consultancy delivering solutions across the globe. In 2016 they rebranded and went through a significant period of growth and recruitment. A move to new headquarters in Oxford presented an ideal opportunity to invest in their team and ensure their people strategy was aligned with the corporate brand strategy.

The senior team was clear that following this period of growth, they wanted to achieve a consistently high standard of professionalism for their clients. It was important to have consultants who could adapt to the changing environment and growing client base. Their consultants needed to be able to quickly build rapport to build trust, be flexible to meet the varied client portfolio and also retain their independence as consultants.

It was key that their professional image, behaviour and communication reflected their ability level but also allowed them to blend into the client environment. We had many useful discussions on appropriate dress codes for each of their clients, whose own dress codes vary from formal business to smart casual.

Mark Bilney, director at OEE, told us, 'Since putting the team through the programme we have noticed a raised collective consciousness around how we interact with our clients. We are focusing much more on mirroring and matching, particularly in terms of dress and deportment. This is helping the team to build rapport quickly with stakeholders positioned at all levels within our clients' organisations.'

What professional image is appropriate in your organisation?

Mastering the art of professional image is a key component of building trust. Getting it wrong can really damage your credibility; getting it right can take you one step closer to finding your T-Spot.

In your workbook you will find a self-audit. Check how you score on professional image skills.
www.firstimpressions.uk.com/trusted/

Credibility sleuth

- Wear clothes that make you feel more confident.

- Think of your working clothes as an investment in your future success; spend the most on the items you will wear most often.

- Determine how to reflect the brand image of the organisation you work for.

- Consider how much authority or approachability you need to display to ensure your message is congruent with your visual appearance.

- Be considerate of your client's dress code.

- Consider the colours you wear and how you might use the psychology of colour to help communicate your message.

- Be aware of dressing for your body shape, scale and proportion.

- Always be immaculately groomed; hair, nails, clothes, shoes and accessories all need to be well cared for, whatever the dress code for the occasion.

- Express your individuality within your organisation's dress code.

 Credibility thief

- We all have a personal brand, whether we consider it or not—don't let yours happen by accident.

- Buying large quantities of cheap clothing will work against you.

- Your personal brand shouldn't clash with the brand image of the organisation you work for.

- Don't display authority if it isn't necessary.

- Getting the dress code wrong for prospect or client meetings may mean that you don't get a second chance.

- Don't be too casual or scruffy on dress-down days—consider the potential impact on your performance.

- If clothes are too big or too small for you, you will look bigger than you really are.

- Ill-fitting clothes, poor grooming and lack of attention to detail will rob you of your credibility.

- Avoid anything distracting or dramatic.

Moving forward

 We hope that you are now much clearer on how to introduce the credibility sleuth into your practices, and that you are looking out for the 1% marginal gains. You will have likely picked up some ideas on how to improve the relationships you have with your clients. By implementing the strategies we've suggested, you will become an advocate for your organisation; your internal culture will improve, your reputation will improve and, in turn, your company profits will increase.

Human relationships are complex, and we should be mindful of the time they take to build and maintain. Relationship management happens in the moment, and at times it can be quite stressful, especially when deadlines are looming and workloads are high. Despite the development of artificial intelligence, the intricacies of human relationships can't be completely replaced by a robot—nor would we want them to be.

 Always watch out for the credibility thief: he has the ability to show up at any time. If he does, take action immediately to minimise the impact on your reputation and your bottom line.

HAVE YOU FOUND YOUR T-SPOT?

This isn't a quick fix or a one-off fix. Cultural and behavioural transformation takes time and focus. It requires clear purpose, vision and values that everyone in the organisation lives by. When you consistently reward the behaviours that reinforce these values, transformation will take place.

Developing yourself and your people in the five key areas of the T-Spot Model will bring you and your business closer to finding the elusive T-Spot, where trusted relationships reside.

Practising a small set of principles on a consistent basis will result in renewed energy within your organisation.

Success comes with discipline and persistence.

The more we develop our relationship-building skills, and the more we all share our knowledge and help others, the stronger our relationships will become. If what you have read has inspired you, please pass on your new knowledge and share our book so it can inspire others.

'Business is about keeping your customers happy and keeping your employees happy.'
– Ron Zambonini, former CEO of Cognos

Remember to visit our website for further helpful resources and a workbook to download: www.firstimpressions.uk.com/trusted
www.firstimpressions.uk.com/trusted

Bringing *Trusted* to your organisation

So now you have an idea of what it takes to build outstanding client relationships, and you have identified where you can make your 1% improvements for an aggregation of marginal gains. What about your colleagues within your immediate team or the wider organisation?

If you would like to see culture change transformation in your organisation, First Impressions delivers an extensive range of keynotes, bespoke programmes, public programmes, team days, facilitation and one-to-one coaching to meet your needs. We work with leaders through to graduates to ensure the change is embedded.

Here are some examples of programmes we offer. This isn't an exhaustive list; through an understanding of your values, your challenges and your people, we can develop bespoke interventions for you.

CULTURE TRANSFORMATION: TURNING YOUR COMPANY VALUES INTO BEHAVIOURS AND SKILLS

Full-day interactive programme. It's not what you do, it's how you do it. Learn how to model behaviour of great organisations. Have the courage to understand your own shortcomings and develop an action plan to become a star.

INSPIRING EXCELLENCE TO DELIVER AN OUTSTANDING CLIENT EXPERIENCE

Full-day interactive programme. Service excellence through the lens of the client. Developing service-aptitude skills and non-negotiable standards for the organisation to improve the client experience.

MANAGING YOUR MINDSET FOR SUCCESS

Full-day interactive programme. Learning mindset management techniques and how to develop strategies to perform at your best. How to handle difficult situations and challenges without getting stressed.

UNDERSTANDING AND FLEXING YOUR COMMUNICATION STYLE

Half- or full-day interactive programme. Gain an understanding of DiSC® behavioural profiling to improve productivity, teamwork and communication. Learn a common language to help teams understand themselves and others at a deeper level.

BEHAVIOUR AND ETIQUETTE IN BUSINESS

Half- or full-day interactive programme. Practical programme on how to conduct yourself in business in any situation and the behaviours needed to get ahead.

MAKING A POSITIVE IMPACT THROUGH YOUR PERSONAL BRAND

Half- or full-day interactive programme. Understand image as a key communication skill; learn how to create impact through personal brand management. Develop the skills to reinforce your organisation's values through your personal presentation.

NETWORKING FOR BUSINESS GROWTH

Half- or full-day interactive programme. Practical session covering all aspects of networking, from planning and preparation to handling nerves, working the room, questioning techniques and follow-up.

For more information, please visit our website or drop us a line:

www.firstimpressions.uk.com
enquiries@firstimpressions.uk.com

Join us on Facebook, LinkedIn and Twitter

Facebook: www.facebook.com/FirstImpressionsTraining/
Twitter: www.twitter.com/FstImpressions
LinkedIn: www.linkedin.com/in/lynb2/
www.linkedin.com/in/donnawhitbrook/

Acknowledgements

We are so grateful to everyone who helped and supported us with the creation of this book. Completing the task from start to finish in six months alongside our usual day jobs was no mean feat. It was made possible by the support we received from those around us.

We loved working together on the book, and that really kept us going. It was both challenging and rewarding in equal measure.

Special thanks go to Nigel Bromley (Lyn's husband) for being an excellent sounding board, our fiercest critic and our biggest cheerleader!

Our teenagers, Harvey Wedgbury and Gracie Bromley, had to raise their game and become more independent while we were preoccupied with writing! They also provided valuable information from their perspective as young adults, and they provided inspiration in bucket loads.

Our wider circle of family and friends, including mentoring group Fit For Business, has been fantastic, and must be fed up by now of hearing the word 'Trusted'!

Our fabulous writing coach and publisher, Alison Jones, was always on hand to answer our daft questions and reassure us that we were on the right path. We have been inspired by her weekly podcast: The Extraordinary Business Book Club. We have gained valuable insights and tips that helped us in writing our book. Thank you, Alison.

extraordinarybusinessbooks.com/

We received invaluable feedback from our beta readers, and their feedback informed the shaping of the book.

Huge thanks go to our expert contributors for sharing inspiring stories with us that add real substance to the book. We have listed them all below.

Beta readers

Lucy Barton
Dr Denise Taylor
Sarah Jordan / Natalie Ormerod
Jan Carrington
Nigel Bromley
Mark Moseley
Henrik Court
Andrew Haworth
Beryl Reeves
Anthony Dugmore
Mike Quinn
Kate Davies

Element 1: Mindset

Mark Cadwallader, Regional Director, Lloyds Bank
Hannah Alexander, Area Director, Lloyds Bank
Mandy Cooper, CEO, Bayberry Clinics
Steve Fleming, CEO, Birmingham Optical Group Ltd
Natalie Ormerod, Head of HR and Quality, Band Hatton Button Solicitors
Andrew Haworth, Managing Director, Bartle Hall Hotel
Caroline Suggett, Executive Coach and Mindfulness Teacher

Element 2: Communication

Hannah Alexander, Area Director of SME Banking, Lloyds Banking Group

Priscilla Morris, Voice Coach, Loud & Clear

Mark Moseley, Managing Director, Band Hatton Button Solicitors

Kathryn Clarke, Personal Branding & Communication Strategist

Element 3: Interaction

Sarah Windrum, CEO, Emerald Group

Oliver Buckle, former Head of Marketing, Else Solicitors

Steve Fleming, CEO, Birmingham Optical Group Ltd

Pete Hall, Managing Director, 2 Blues Ltd

Henrik Court, Marketing and Networking Professional

Paul Brown, Head of Public Sector Audit, EY

Nicola Millard, Head of Customer Insight and Futures, BT

Element 4: Behaviour

Nigel Bromley, Client Services Director, Key Parker

Tara Robinson, Sales and Marketing Director, The Eden Hotel Collection

Lauren Ward, Management Trainee, Nationwide Building Society

Lucy Barton, Senior Membership Value Propositions Manager, Nationwide Building Society

Andrew Haworth, Managing Director, Bartle Hall Hotel

Dominic Myles, former European Services Leader, IBM

Tony Davis, former CEO, Bmibaby Ltd

Sarah Windrum, CEO, Emerald Group

Elinor Perry, Managing Director, Pentlands Accountants and Business Advisors

Element 5: Professional image

Mark Bilney, Director, OEE Consulting
Paul Campion and Julia Campion, previous co-owners of
First Impressions

General

Abby Wilkes, Personal Branding Photographer, Abby Wilkes
Photography
Sarah Shakouri, Photographer, Honou Photography
Michelle Abrahall, Designer, Michelle Abrahall
Rachel Small, Editor, Faultless Finish Editing
Helen McCusker, Book Publicist, Bookollective

References and research

Introduction

- M. Weinberger, in Legends Report article by J. Singh. Available from www.legends.report/ey-ernst-young-ceo-a-cup-of-coffee-is-worth-more-than-1000-tweets/ [accessed 28 February 2017].

- R. Branson, Virgin (2014). Available from www.virgin.com/richard-branson/look-after-your-staff [accessed 2 April 2017].

- J. Kotter and J. Heskett, *Corporate Culture and Performance* (1992).

- J. Clear (on Sir David Brailsford), *This coach improved every tiny thing by 1% and here's what happened*, James Clear (2017). Available from jamesclear.com/marginal-gains [accessed 6 January 2017].

- BBC News (on Sir David Brailsford), *Viewpoint: should we all be looking for marginal gains*, BBC News (2015). Available from www.bbc.co.uk/news/magazine-34247629 [accessed 6 January 2017].

- A. Einstein, Quote Addicts (2017). Available from quoteaddicts.com/i/146231 [accessed 20 January 2017].

- J. Olson, *The Slight Edge* (2013).

Mindset

- S. Tzu, Goodreads (2017). Available from www.goodreads. com/quotes/79599-know-yourself-and-you-will-win-all-battles [accessed 1 September 2017].

- H. Ford, Goodreads (2017). Available from www.goodreads. com/quotes/978-whether-you-think-you-can-or-you-think-you-can-t--you-re [accessed 12 February 2017].

- C. S. Dweck, *Mindset* (Updated edition) (2017).

- C. Fong, in 12 *habits of genuine people*, by T. Bradberry, Forbes (2016). Available from www.forbes.com/sites/ travisbradberry/2016/05/10/12-habits-of-genuine-people/ [accessed 4 March 2017].

- Z. Bulygo, *Tony Hsieh, Zappos and the art of great company culture*, Kissmetrics Blog (2017). Available from blog. kissmetrics.com/zappos-art-of-culture/ [accessed 25 May 2017].

- T. Bradberry and J. Greaves, *Emotional Intelligence 2.0* (2009).

- D. Golman, M. Elias, G. Bharwaney, H. Riess, J. Meyer, C. Cherniss and M. Brackett, Consortium for Research on Emotional Intelligence in Organizations (2017). Available from www.eiconsortium.org [accessed 20 February 2017].

- L. Graziano Breuning, *Habits of a Happy Brain* (2015).

- UK Government Health and Safety Executive, *Work related stress, anxiety and depression statistics in Great Britain 2016*, Health and Safety Executive (2016). Available from www.hse.gov.uk/statistics/causdis/stress/ [accessed 14 April 2017].

- R. Bandler. Awaken (2012). Available from www.awaken. com/2012/11/quotes-by-richard-bandler/ [accessed 21 January 2017].

- M. Williams, in *Mindfulness*, NHS Choices (2016). Available from www.nhs.uk/Conditions/stress-anxiety-depression/pages/mindfulness.aspx [accessed 7 April 2017].
- A. Cuddy, *Your body language may shape who you are*, TED.com (2017). Available from www.ted.com/talks/amy_cuddy_your_body_language_shapes_who_you_are [accessed 6 Jan 2017].

Communication

- J. Haley, *Conversations with Milton H. Erickson MD: Changing Individuals v.1* (2013).
- M. Mehl, in 'Why We Should Be Having More Meaningful Conversations', by J. Grenneman, *Psychology Today* (2017). Available from www.psychologytoday.com/blog/the-secret-lives-introverts/201706/why-we-should-be-having-more-meaningful-conversations [accessed on 24 June 2017].
- BBC News, *Terminally ill doctor Kate Granger's 'my name is' campaign wins support*, BBC News (2015). Available from www.bbc.co.uk/news/health-31062042 [accessed 21 March 2017].
- A. Pentland, *Honest Signals* (2010).
- P. Ekman, *Emotions Revealed* (2004).
- W. F. Chaplin et al., 'Personality processes and individual differences—handshaking, gender, personality, and first impressions' in *Journal of Personality and Social Psychology* 79, 110–117 (2000). Available from www.apa.org/pubs/journals/releases/psp791110.pdf [accessed on 14 January 2017].

- F. Dolcos et al., 'The power of a handshake: Neural correlates of evaluative judgements in observed social interactions' in *Journal of Cognitive Neuroscience* 24 (12) (2012). Available from www.mitpressjournals.org/doi/pdf/10.1162/jocn_a_00295 [accessed on 7 January 2017].
- S. R. Covey, *The 7 Habits of Highly Effective People* (1989).
- A. J. C. Cuddy, C. A. Wilmuth and D. R. Carney, 'The benefit of power posing before a high-stakes social evaluation', *Harvard Business School Working Paper 13-027* (2012). Available from dash.harvard.edu/bitstream/handle/1/9547823/13-027.pdf?sequence=1 [accessed 4 February 2017].
- A. Pease and B. Pease, *The Definitive Book of Body Language* (2006).
- M. Argyle and J. Dean, 'Eye contact, distance and affiliation' in *Sociometry*, 28 (3), 289–304 (1965). Available from www.columbia.edu/~rmk7/HC/HC_Readings/Argyle.pdf [accessed 7 March 2017].
- A. Robbins, *Awaken the Giant Within* (2001).
- P. Morris, Loud & Clear (2017). Available from www.loudandclearuk.com/ [accessed 20 May 2017].

Interaction

- Z. Ziglar and J. P. Hayes, *Network Marketing for Dummies* (2011).
- J. C. Wong, 'Uber CEO Travis Kalanick caught on video arguing with driver about fares', *The Guardian* (2017). Available from www.theguardian.com/technology/2017/feb/28/uber-ceo-travis-kalanick-driver-argument-video-fare-prices [accessed on 5 May 2017].
- J. R. DiJulius III, *What's the Secret* (2008).

- N. J. Millard, *The collaboration conudrum*, BT Global Services (2016). Available from www.globalservices. bt.com/uk/en/point-of-view/the-collaboration-conundrum [accessed 2 March 2017].

- E. Jones and N. Millard, *The changing face of business relationships* (2015). Available from business.bt.com/ content/dam/bt/business/Business-Solutions/Downloads-PDF/see-what-happens-report.pdf [accessed 2 March 2017].

- J. Mercola, *The power of face-to-face meetings in a digital world*, Mercola (2015). Available from articles.mercola.com/ sites/articles/archive/2015/10/08/face-to-face-meetings. aspx [accessed on 20 June 2017].

- J. Jiang, B. Dai, D. Peng, C. Zhu, L. Liu and C. MingLu, 'Neural synchronisation during face-to-face communication' in *Journal of Neuroscience*, 32 (45) 16064–16069 (2012). DOI: doi.org/10.1523/JNEUROSCI.2926-12.2012

- A. Pentland, 'Betting on people power' in MIT IDE research brief 12 (2016). Available from ide.mit.edu/sites/default/ files/publications/IDE%20Research%20Brief_v12%20 Sandy%20Pentland.pdf [accessed on 7 June 2017].

- E. Hallowell, 'The human moment at work', *Harvard Business Review* (1999). Available from hbr.org/1999/01/ the-human-moment-at-work [accessed on 23 August 2017].

- S. Edinger, 'Three elements of great communication, according to Aristotle', *Harvard Business Review* (2013). Available from hbr.org/2013/01/three-elements-of-great-communication-according [accessed on 11 June 2017].

- S. Sinek, *Start with Why* (2009).

- T. Cram, *The Finishing Touch* (2010).

- J. C. Maxwell, *Winning with People* (2011).

- A. Cuddy, *Presence* (2016)

- *JFK and the Janitor: the importance of understanding the WHY that is behind what we do*, beqom Blog (2014). Available from www.beqom.com/US-en/blog/jfk-and-the-janitor-the-importance-of-understanding-the-why [accessed on 4 May 2017].

Behaviour

- M. Angelou, *I Know Why the Caged Bird Sings* (1969).
- T. Yaffe and R. Kark, 'Leading by example: The case of leader OCB' in *Journal of Applied Psychology* (doi 10.1037/a0022464) (2011). Available from www.researchgate.net/publication/50890447_Leading_by_example_The_case_of_leader_OCB [accessed on 14 June 2017].
- A. Einstein. Working Minds. Available from www.working-minds.com/AEquotes.htm?Albert-Einstein [accessed on 23 June 2017].
- *Culture at Netflix*, Netflix, Inc.. Available from jobs.netflix.com/culture/#introduction [accessed 23 July 2017].
- B. L. Simmons, 'Evidence for leading by example', *Bret L. Simmons—Positive Organizational Behavior* (2011). Available from www.bretlsimmons.com/2011-04/evidence-for-leading-by-example/ [accessed on 6 May 2017].
- E. Anderson, C. Fornell and D. Lehmann, 'Customer satisfaction, market share, and profitability: Findings from Sweden' in *Journal of Marketing* 58, 53–66 (1994). Available from www.jstor.org/stable/1252310?seq=1#page_scan_tab_contents [accessed on 6 March 2017].
- J. R. DiJulius III, *What's the Secret* (2008).
- B. Thompson, 'Take a tip from Bezos: Customers always need a seat at the table'. *Entrepreneur*. Available from www.entrepreneur.com/article/234254 [accessed on 14 June 2017].

- Nationwide Building Society, *Our PRIDE statement*. Available from www.nationwide-jobs.co.uk/why-work-for-us/our-values/our-pride-statement/ [accessed on 8 April 2017].

Professional image

- H. Adam and A. Galinsky, 'Enclothed Cognition' in *Journal of Experimental Social Psychology* (2012). Available from digitalintelligencetoday.com/wp-content/uploads/2015/11/2012-Enclothed-Cognition.pdf [accessed 9 January 2017].

- C. Jarrett, 'Introducing "Enclothed Cognition" —how what we wear affects how we think' in *British Psychological Society Research Digest* (2012). Available from digest.bps.org.uk/2012/03/01/introducing-enclothed-cognition-how-what-we-wear-affects-how-we-think/ [accessed on 27 January 2017].

- K. Pine, *Mind What You Wear: The Psychology of Fashion* (2014).

- M. Hutson and T. Rodriguez, 'Dress for success: How clothes influence our performance', *Scientific American* (2016). Available from www.scientificamerican.com/article/dress-for-success-how-clothes-influence-our-performance/ [accessed 18 January 2017].

- P. and J. Campion, *Cycle of Success* (2004).

- A. R. Timming, 'Visible tattoos in the service sector: A new challenge to recruitment and selection' in *Work, Employment and Society* 29 (1), 60–78 (2015). Available from risweb.st-andrews.ac.uk/portal/en/researchoutput/visible-tattoos-in-the-service-sector(0e2e39f4-4035-4e1c-bbb5-824018c4caf0).html [accessed 4 March 2017].

- A. R. Timming, *Having a visible tattoo can help job seekers find employment, research says*, British Sociological Association (2016). Available from www.britsoc.co.uk/about/latest-news/2016/september/having-a-visible-tattoo-can-help-job-seekers-find-employment-research-says/ [accessed 5 May 2017].

- House of Commons Petitions Committee and Women and Equalities Committee, *High heels and workplace dress codes* HC 291 (2017). Available from publications.parliament.uk/pa/cm201617/cmselect/cmpetitions/291/291.pdf [accessed on 2 February 2017].

- Social Mobility Commission, *Socio-Economic Diversity in Life Sciences and Investment Banking* (2016). Available from www.gov.uk/government/uploads/system/uploads/attachment_data/file/549994/Socio-economic_diversity_in_life_sciences_and_investment_banking.pdf [accessed on 20 January 2017].

Recommended further reading

Introduction

- John P. Kotter and James L. Heskett, *Corporate Culture and Performance* (updated 2011).
- Jeff Olson, *The Slight Edge: Turning Simple Disciplines into Massive Success and Happiness* (2013).

Mindset

- Dr Carol S. Dweck, *Mindset: The New Psychology of Success* (updated 2017).
- Daniel Goleman, *Emotional Intelligence: Why It Can Matter More Than IQ* (1996).
- Travis Bradberry and Jean Greaves, *Emotional Intelligence 2.0* (2010).
- Loretta Graziano Breuning, PhD, *Habits of a Happy Brain: Retrain Your Brain to Boost Your Serotonin, Dopamine, Oxytocin, & Endorphin Levels* (2015).
- Mark Williams and Danny Penman, *Mindfulness: A Practical Guide to Finding Peace in a Frantic World* (2011).

Communication

- Alex (Sandy) Pentland, *Honest Signals: How They Shape Our World* (updated 2010).

- Paul Ekman, *Emotions Revealed: Recognizing Faces and Feelings to Improve Communication and Emotional life* (2004).

- Amy Cuddy, *Presence: Bringing Your Boldest Self to Your Biggest Challenges* (2016).

- Sue Knight, *NLP at Work: The Essence of Excellence, 3rd Edition (People Skills for Professionals)* (updated 2009).

- Judi James, *BodyTalk at Work: How to Use Effective Body Language to Boost Your Career* (2001).

- Allan and Barbara Pease, *The Definitive Book of Body Language: How to Read Others' Attitudes by Their Gestures* (updated 2017).

Interaction

- Edward M. Hallowell, *Human Moments: How to Find Meaning and Love in Your Everyday Life* (2003).

- Simon Sinek, *Start With Why: How Great Leaders Inspire Everyone to Take Action* (2011).

- Tony Cram, *The Finishing Touch: How to Build World-Class Customer Service* (2010).

- Will Kintish, *Business Networking—The Survival Guide: How to Make Networking Less about Stress and More about Success* (2014).

Behaviour

- Barbara Pachter, *The Essentials of Business Etiquette: How to Greet, Eat, and Tweet Your Way to Success* (2013).
- Simon Sinek, *Leaders Eat Last: Why Some Teams Pull Together and Others Don't* (updated 2017).

Professional image

- Professor Karen J. Pine, *Mind What You Wear: The Psychology of Fashion* (2014).

About the authors

impressions

First Impressions Training Ltd

Established in 1984, the business has consistently evolved to meet the needs of our clients and now offers a comprehensive set of disciplines covering all aspects of people development, leadership, culture transformation and world-class service delivery.

First Impressions began as an image consultancy and grew to become a people development organisation that currently spans the UK, Europe and Asia.

We continue to help our clients to manage their personal impact ensuring it is appropriate, consistent and memorable.

We pride ourselves on quickly getting to the heart of business challenges and providing bespoke solutions for our clients. Our work ranges from one-to-one coaching or small group consultations through to presentations, seminars and interactive programmes at all levels within organisations.

In today's world of work, being competent and doing a really good job is simply not enough. Today we must have the ability to create impact and maximise our personal presence in order to be positively memorable. Being a brand ambassador for our business and being able to engage with others confidently in order to build successful, professional relationships is key to outstanding performance.

First Impressions supports and works closely with the charity Look Good Feel Better, and gets involved in supporting Young Enterprise and The Peter Jones Enterprise Academy. Managing Director Lyn Bromley has judged Young Enterprise for three years and has been involved in supporting budding entrepreneurs at the academy. We also support, guide and advise Suited for Success and Sport 4 Life, two charities that help people create a brighter working future.

Lyn Bromley has been the managing director of First Impressions Training Ltd since September 2010.

She is an experienced people manager, trainer and consultant. Her wide-ranging corporate background spans finance, training, consultancy and project management. She held senior leadership positions and has worked with clients from a whole host of industries, from financial services to law, from SMEs to blue chip organisations.

 Donna Whitbrook is an experienced corporate consultant and people developer. Her extensive corporate background spans finance, training, consultancy, performance improvement, governance and strategy.

She has held senior management positions in banking and finance and board-level positions in the public and third sectors.

Lyn and Donna have a real belief in the work they promote. They are passionate about developing leaders and helping businesses to transform the performance of their individuals and teams, enabling them to reflect their organisation's brand vision and values and deliver world-class service to their valued clients.

Index

A

B

C

E

F

G

H

Lightning Source UK Ltd.
Milton Keynes UK
UKOW06f1507031117
312045UK00007B/29/P